discover Cardiff

five historical walks around the city

By Liz Unwin

Illustrations by Mary Unwin & others

Edited by Geoff Stickler
Published by Cardiff Marketing Ltd

First published in 1995 by
Cardiff Marketing Ltd
PO Box 48
Cardiff, Wales
CF1 1XQ

Printed in Wales by
Hackman Printers,
Ynyshir, Porth, Rhondda

CONTENTS

ACKNOWLEDGEMENTS

Many thanks to all those friends and acquaintances who have given me encouragement and helped with the compilation of this book, in particular:-

For the lovely pen and ink drawings:
my very talented mum, Mary Unwin.

For proof reading and advice on technical writing:
Clive 'King Comma' Turner, Kate Daugela, Jane Jones.

For trying out the walks:
Chris Allender, Chris Breen, Hilary Fairney and Pip the dog, Julie Harrington-Bond, Duncan Innes, Dani Jackson, Claire Leopold, Vitty Piatti, Gary Reynolds, Daniel & Tanya Thomas, Chris Wallace, Dave & Fiona Wynford-Thomas

For extra information:
Anne Jones (Cardiff City Council's Leisure and Amenities Department), Phillip Riden (University of Wales College Cardiff, Department of Extra-Mural Studies), Muriel Jeremy (Llandaff Society).

For access to word processing and printing facilities:
Stephen Palmer, Chris Wallace.

For Welsh translation:
Rhiân Huws (University of Wales College, Cardiff).

For advice on publishing:
Susan Jenkins (University of Wales Press), Peter Finch (Oriel).

For encouragement and help with ALL aspects of the book:
Chris Wallace.

And last, but by no means least, thanks to Jane and Norman Jones for putting me up (and putting up with me) whenever I'm in Cardiff, and without whom none of this would be possible.

LIST OF ILLUSTRATIONS

The illustrations/photographs on pages marked with an asterisk are reproduced courtesy of Cardiff Central Library.

INTRODUCTION

Cardiff is a beautiful city, with a Civic Centre acclaimed as one of the finest in Europe, and more than two thousand acres of parkland. This is more green space per head of population than any other city in Europe.

I fell in love with Cardiff when I came to the University of Wales Institute of Science and Technology in 1981. However, as often happens, I never quite got around to exploring the immediate vicinity.

The idea for this book arose quite by accident - literally - when my car was written off by an uninsured driver. Now that I was grounded this seemed as good a time as any to explore the area around Cardiff. I looked around for a book of guided walks but at the time there were none available - so I decided to write my own.

As the book progressed I became more interested in the history of Cardiff, and the theme of the book changed to reflect this. Consequently, the areas covered in these walks have been chosen for their historical importance in the development of Cardiff. I hope that the walks bring the historical facts to life and help you to find your way around the city.

Although an Ordnance Survey map of the area is not necessary, the walks in this book can be found on the Landranger 171 OS map and a grid reference is given for the starting points. Three of the walks begin from Cardiff Castle, which is in the centre of the city, and the starting points of the other two are easily accessible by public transport.

All the walks are circular and range in length from 1.5 to 5.5 miles (3.2 to 8.8km), although the two longer walks can be shortened by doing a linear walk and catching a bus back into town. The routes, which have been tried and tested at least twice by myself, and by a 'volunteer' with little knowledge of Cardiff to ensure that the instructions are clear and easy to follow, have been cunningly designed to incorporate a place of refreshment, i.e. a pub, along the way.

Cardiff today is one of Britain's top tourist centres, visited by over two million visitors each year. It is a bustling, cosmopolitan city, renowned for its shopping facilities. However, if you take the time to try the walks in this book you will discover a very different Cardiff - an ancient city, steeped in history.

Liz Unwin

John Crichton Stuart, Second Marquis of Bute

A BRIEF HISTORY OF CARDIFF

The history of Cardiff began with the Romans, who arrived in the area about AD 50 and defeated the Silures, a fierce Celtic tribe who inhabited South Wales at that time. The early history of the city is inextricably bound up with the history of Cardiff Castle.

Cardiff Castle

The Romans built the first fort in Cardiff, a ten-acre stronghold, at a strategic point on the River Taff, where the river could be forded. By AD 75 the Romans controlled all of Wales and rebuilt the fort, making it considerably smaller. During a troubled period, about AD 250, the fort was rebuilt again, this time with ten feet thick walls, backed by an earth bank and surrounded by a moat. The Roman parts of the present castle wall can still be seen, outlined with red Radyr stone.

The Romans left in the fifth century and little is known about the inhabitants of the area until the Normans arrived in the eleventh century. Robert Fitzhamon, the Norman Lord of Gloucester, who defeated Iestyn ap Gwrgan, Prince of Glamorgan, in 1091, used the strategic site of the old Roman fort to build his medieval castle. In the north-west corner he built a keep. This consisted of a forty feet high mound, surrounded by a moat. On top of the mound, the Lord and his household lived in wooden buildings enclosed by a timber stockade. Later, in the twelfth century, the wooden keep was replaced with a twelve-sided stone keep with six feet thick walls. This keep still stands today, dominating the castle grounds.

The Normans enlarged and deepened the Roman ditch around the outer defences, throwing the excavated soil over the curtain walls. The soil covered the Roman walls, which were not discovered until the Norman bank was excavated by the Third Marquis of Bute in the nineteenth century. Because they had been protected from the elements for so long, the walls were in an excellent state of preservation. A 270 feet long portion of Roman wall is on display inside the castle grounds.

The Norman Keep

Lords of the castle lived in the keep from the eleventh to the fifteenth century, but Welsh attacks meant that the castle had to be strengthened and improved. After the final defeat of the turbulent Welsh Prince, Owain Glyndwr, in the fifteenth century, came a more settled period, enabling new residential and administrative buildings to be built along the west curtain wall. Further additions were made to the castle in Tudor and Stuart times.

Cardiff became involved in the English Civil War of 1642, and the castle was held first by the Royalists and later by the Parliamentarians. Years of decay followed and the castle fell into disrepair until the Bute family inherited the estate in the eighteenth century. The First

Marquis of Bute engaged 'Capability' Brown and Harry Holland to landscape the grounds and modernise the accommodation for his son. However, when his son died in 1794 at the age of twenty-seven, the Marquis lost interest in the project. The Second Marquis of Bute did some improvements to the castle but it was not until the nineteenth century, when the Third Marquis appointed the architect William Burges, that the castle was really transformed.

The Industrial Revolution

By the end of the thirteenth century Cardiff's population had reached 2,000. Although Cardiff grew in importance during the sixteenth and seventeenth centuries, the population remained stable until the industrial revolution of the nineteenth century. During the years of the industrial revolution Cardiff experienced phenomenal growth, largely due to the discovery of iron and coal in the valleys to the north.

There were three main phases to Cardiff's growth. The first phase began with the opening of the Glamorganshire Canal in 1794, to transport iron from Merthyr to Cardiff. Horse-drawn waggons were replaced by barges, which could carry up to twelve times more iron. The growth triggered by the Canal lasted until about 1840, by which time the population of Cardiff had increased to more than 10,000.

The second phase of growth was brought about by the opening of Cardiff's first dock, the Bute West Dock, and the Taff Vale Railway. By the time the Bute West Dock was opened, in 1839, the Glamorganshire Canal had already become incapable of meeting the transport demands placed upon it by the expanding iron and coal industries in the valleys. A railway was proposed, and in 1840 the first important railway in Wales, the Taff Vale Railway, was opened from Cardiff to Abercynon. This was extended the following year to Merthyr, and later to Aberdare. Another factor in the growth of the town at this time was due to the Irish potato famine of 1845. Vast numbers of Irish, hoping to find employment in Cardiff, were brought across on the ships as ballast.

The third phase began about 1870 with the growth of coal mining and its exploitation in the Rhondda Valley. In 1871 the borough's population was 39,500 and coal exports were nearly two million tons per year. By 1901 both the population and the coal exports had quadrupled. Coal exports reached their peak in 1913, when ten and a half million tons were exported from Cardiff. At that time Cardiff was the largest coal port in the world.

The Bute Family

No history of Cardiff is complete without mentioning the Butes. This family, of Scottish ancestry, transformed Cardiff from an insignificant town into the capital city of Wales. The Bute's association with Cardiff began in 1766, when Charlotte Windsor, heiress to the Herbert and Windsor estates, married John, Lord Mountstuart, the eldest son of the Prime Minister, Lord Bute. With the marriage came Cardiff Castle, estates in Cardiff, and mineral rights for vast areas in the valleys. Lord Mountstuart was made the First Marquis of Bute in 1796, but he was a rakish character who did little for Cardiff.

The 'Father of modern Cardiff' was his grandson, who became the Second Marquis of Bute in 1814 at the age of twenty. He was a generous patron of local charities and causes, especially education, and much respected in Cardiff. He was also a ruthless and hard-working businessman, and added to the Bute Estate. In the 1830s he risked his fortune to build Cardiff's first dock, the Bute West Dock, to provide an outlet for the iron and coal being mined in the valleys. This was the first of a series of docks and laid the foundations for Cardiff's phenomenal growth. He died in 1848, leaving a baby son who was to become the Third Marquis.

The Third Marquis, who came of age in 1868, also contributed to the town's development. Unlike his father, he was scholarly, cultured, and deeply religious, and, being the second richest man in Britain, he could afford to indulge his interests. He studied many languages, the scriptures, medieval history, heraldry, art, and archaeology - excavating the sites of the Roman fort, Blackfriars, and Greyfriars in Cardiff. His main passion though was building, and he employed the architect William Burges, an eccentric genius who shared the Marquis's love for all things medieval, to restore Cardiff Castle and Castell Coch to the splendour that we see today. In 1891 the Third Marquis served as Mayor of Cardiff.

Both the Second and Third Marquises were generous benefactors, providing the land for many parks in the town, and preserving acres of parkland in the centre of Cardiff to create a 'countryside within the town' effect. The Third Marquis's last major contribution to Cardiff was the sale of Cathays Park to the Corporation as a site for the Civic Centre - now one of the finest in Europe.

After the death of the Third Marquis in 1900 the family's links with the city were never as strong again. The present Marquis of Bute lives on the Isle of Bute in Scotland, although he still has business interests in Cardiff.

Capital Status

In 1905 Cardiff became a city and in 1954, at a conference of Welsh local authorities, Cardiff was voted the capital city of Wales, beating Swansea, Caernarfon, Aberystwyth, and Machynlleth, who also contested the title. Cardiff officially became the capital city of Wales on 20th December 1955.

Despite the criticism that Cardiff is not typically Welsh, it was chosen for three main reasons. Firstly, the city stands on an ancient site dating back to the Roman occupation of Britain and for centuries has had close ties with Llandaff Cathedral, one of the oldest Christian foundations in Wales. Secondly, with the expansion of the coal industry in the nineteenth century, Cardiff became the largest, richest, and most densely populated part of the country. Thirdly, in Cathays Park, Cardiff had a Civic Centre worthy of a capital city, and this was an attribute that none of Cardiff's rivals could match.

So, despite its contemporary appearance, Cardiff has a long and fascinating history. This book can only give a brief outline of its past, but I hope that this will whet your appetite and make you want to discover more.

THE ROUTE OF THE OLD TOWN WALL

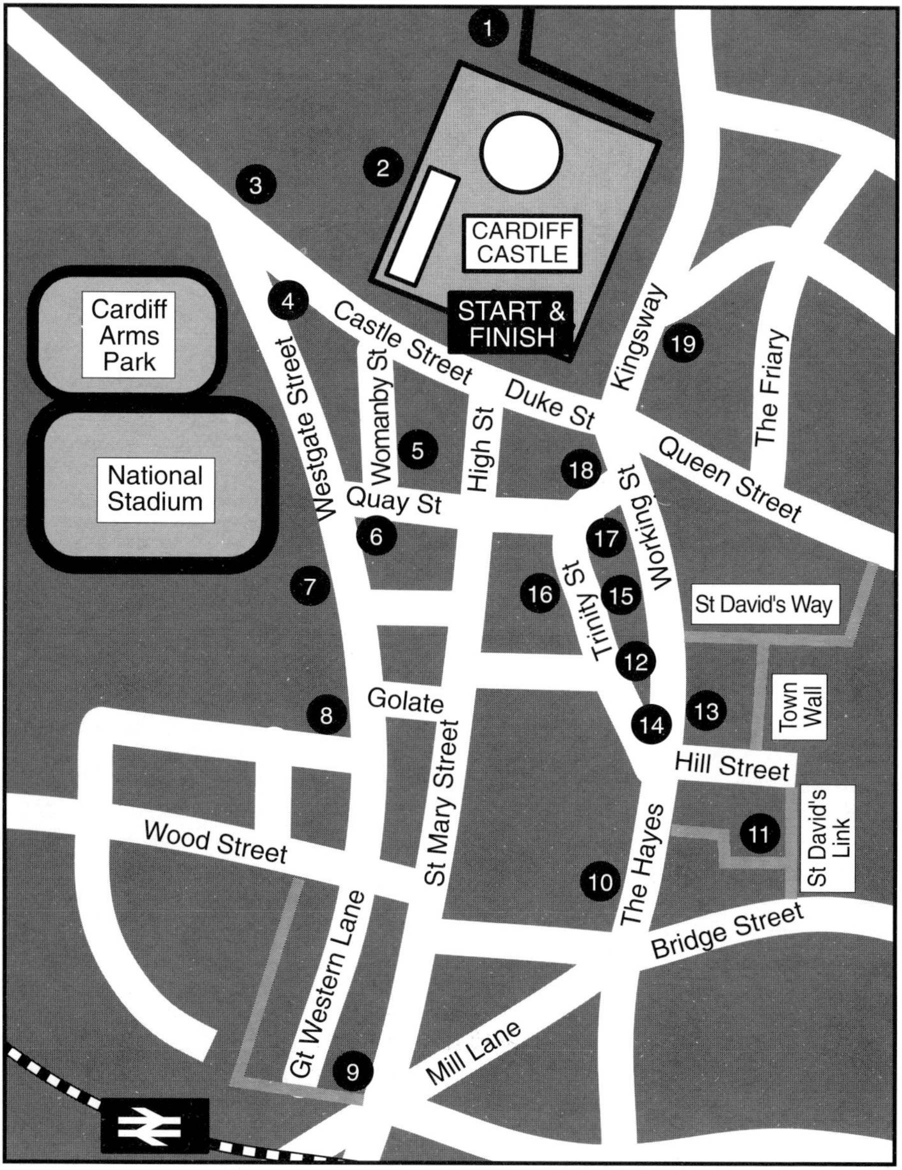

WALK 1
OS Sheet 171. 181 765 - 2 miles (3.2km)

THE CITY CENTRE
THE ROUTE OF THE OLD TOWN WALL

This walk takes you on a circular tour of the city, beginning at Cardiff Castle, and following the route of the old town wall. Today most of the city lies outside the boundary of the old wall, but, in medieval times, anywhere outside the town wall was considered to be rural.

BELOW: Owain Glyndwr (1359-1415) by Alfred Turner, R.B.S. - to be found in Cardiff City Hall

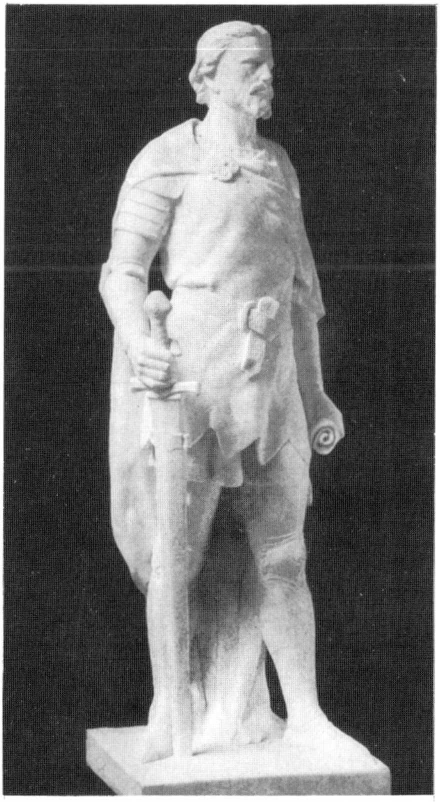

History of the Town Wall

In the eleventh century the Normans arrived in Cardiff. Within a decade of Norman occupation Cardiff had become a borough, a privileged status allowing the Lord to hold markets and collect taxes on goods. This made it commercially important to protect the town so the town wall was built. It is not known exactly when it was built, but it is thought to be the work of Gilbert de Clare in the latter half of the thirteenth century.

The wall, which stood ten feet high and had an average thickness of six to eight feet, was not an adequate defence against major assaults on the town and was damaged several times. The first reported damage to the wall was in 1315 when Llewelyn Bren, a Welsh Prince, attacked Cardiff. The most successful raid was that by Owain Glyndwr, the greatest and most warlike Welsh Prince, in 1404, when much of the town was destroyed. For many decades after this attack tolls were imposed on traders in the town to pay for the repair of the wall.

Although the wall may have acted as some deterrent to raids on the town, its main purpose was to keep intruders out of the borough at night. A curfew was imposed nightly, when gatekeepers closed the six gates which gave access to the town. These were reopened in the morning when the church bells of St. Mary's or St. John's marked the lifting of the curfew.

The town wall gates were removed between 1781 and 1802 to improve access to the town, and the last remains of the wall disappeared in 1901.

Facing the main entrance to Cardiff Castle, turn right and follow the castle wall. Go into Bute Park by the first entrance on your left, near the subway. Follow the path straight on, and cross the bridge over the dock feeder (1).

The dock feeder, which was built in 1834, drew water from the River Taff and carried it to the docks. Here it was used to flush away any mud brought in by the tide, and to maintain the water level.

Take the next path on the left and walk alongside the west side of the castle. Continue until you come to a locked iron gate on your left, where a cobbled drive leads over a bridge to a gateway (2).

This is a replica of the old West Gate of the town wall, built by the Fourth Marquis of Bute in 1921. The West Gate was also known as the Mill Gate because the town mill stood nearby. The main road to Swansea passed through this gate and continued westwards over the bridge across the River Taff, which was about eighty yards upstream from the present bridge. The original West Gate was demolished in 1781 to widen the road and improve access to the town.

Continue along the path to a junction of paths. Turn left here and leave the Park by the gate beside the old Castle Lodge (3).

This small residence was, until recently, the home of the Park keeper.

Turn left and walk past some of the animals on the castle wall.

The Animal Wall was designed by William Burges but built after his death in 1881 by his assistant, William Frame. It was originally situated just outside the south gate of the castle, but after the First World War it was moved to its present position and extended. The additional animals were carved by Alexander Carrick, a Scottish sculptor.

Stop at the pedestrian crossing. To your left, on the opposite side of the road, is Bob Bevan's motorcycle shop.

From the West Gate the wall ran through what is now this shop. It then continued between Westgate Street and Womanby Street.

Cross the road and take the road to the right of the Angel Hotel (4) - Westgate Street.

Formerly called Park Road, Westgate Street stands on the old course of the River Taff, which formed part of the western defences of the town. The river was prone to flooding so this stretch of the town wall was often rebuilt. In 1849, in an attempt to stop the floods, the bend in the river was straightened by Brunel.

The Angel Hotel is the successor of the Cardiff Arms Hotel, one of the most important coaching hotels in Cardiff, which gave its name to the Cardiff Arms Park. The Cardiff Arms Hotel

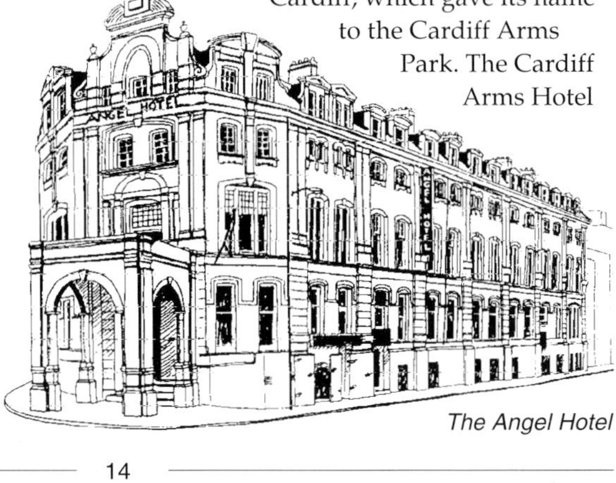

The Angel Hotel

was demolished in 1878 when Castle Street was widened.

On the right, part of the Cardiff Arms Park can be seen.

This site, which used to be known as the Great Park, was acquired by the First Marquis of Bute in 1803. Before the course of the Taff was altered the Park was flooded for much of the time. The diversion not only stopped the flooding but increased the size of the Park, which by then was known as the Cardiff Arms Park. Cricket, football, athletics, and, of course, rugby were played at the ground. In the 1880s the stadium was developed by the Cardiff Football Club and the Welsh Rugby Union. The first international rugby match played at Cardiff Arms Park took place against Ireland in 1884. When the Fourth Marquis of Bute decided to sell the Arms Park in 1922 the flats in Westgate Street were built on part of the land and Cardiff Athletic Club bought the stadium. The Welsh Rugby Union became a major shareholder in the Athletic Club and in the 1960s the Arms Park became the home of Welsh rugby.

Continue along Westgate Street and take the first left, Quay Street.

Here the Romans established a trading post on the Taff estuary in 75 AD, but it was not until about 1263 that a stone quay was built. This was the site of another gate in the town wall which was known as the Wales Gate until the eighteenth century when it was renamed Blount's Gate after its keeper. This gate provided access to the quay from the High Street. In 1770 Blount's Gate was converted into a storehouse and finally demolished in 1785. A blue plaque on the wall of the multi-storey car park in Quay Street gives the history of Blount's Gate.

Here we make a slight detour from the route of the town wall and take the first left off Quay Street into Womanby Street.

Womanby Street used to be a longer street, including Quay Street. The name Womanby has Viking origins and in the thirteenth century it was known as Hundemanby. Opinion is divided about the meaning of this word, but 'dwelling of the keeper of the hounds' and 'the strangers' quarter' have been suggested.

Go into Jones Court (5) on the right.

New building work could not keep pace with Cardiff's population explosion in the nineteenth century, and overcrowded, squalid courts developed in the centre of town. The row of nine terraced cottages in Jones Court was built by the Second Marquis of Bute in 1830 to house his dockworkers. The building facing the gate stands on a site where traces of occupation from the twelfth century have been found, and the buildings on both sides of the gate stand on the former site of the city's weights and measures building. The Court was acquired by Cardiff City Council at the beginning of the twentieth century and has been renovated as offices, which opened in 1982.

Return to Quay Street and walk to the corner of the multi-storey car park (6) nearest Westgate Street.

Here, a small area with railings around it encloses black bricks. These mark the line of the old town wall. Another patch of bricks can be seen by looking through the gaps in the multi-storey car park wall, opposite the door of the Department of Employment.

Continue along Westgate Street. On the right is the attractive building of 'Jackson's' (7).

This night club is housed in premises that opened in 1878 as the Cardiff Racquets and Fives Club. The Club vacated the building in 1924, after which it was used as a youth employment office and named after the Director of Education, John Jackson.

About a hundred yards further on the left is a street called Golate.

This is one of Cardiff's oldest streets and used to be the site of a gate, Gulley Gate or Golate, in the town wall. This gate allowed access to the lower quay from St. Mary Street. There is another blue information plaque at the other end of Golate.

Opposite Golate is the County Court (1904) and next door to this is the old post office (8).

The old post office is a beautiful Gothic-style building with jutting gables and steep roofs. The first trunk line in Britain was opened between Cardiff and Newport in 1881 and the Westgate Street GPO, built in 1896, soon had to be expanded to meet the needs of the telephone section. The main post office moved to Penarth Road in 1986.

Continue to the end of Westgate Street and turn right at Wood Street. Cross the road at the pedestrian crossing and go straight on, beside the shops, to the railway station.

The General Station (now Central Station) was built on reclaimed land after the diversion of the River Taff. One of Cardiff's earliest suburbs, Temperance Town, was developed on the surrounding area to house immigrants. It was called Temperance Town because the landowner, Colonel Wood, after whom Wood Street is named, would not allow the building of public houses. Built in just six years, the area soon became overcrowded and run down.

Near the railway car park on the left was the Water Gate, a watch tower built into the wall to provide warning against sea attack.

Turn left and walk through the railway car park. The first lane on the left is Great Western Lane.

St. Mary's Church used to stand down here, on the east bank of the river, near the junction of Wood Street and St. Mary Street. Established in 1100 by a prior sent from Tewkesbury Abbey, it was the first church in Cardiff. In 1175 the church was enlarged and rebuilt, but it was badly damaged when Owain Glyndwr attacked Glamorgan in the fifteenth century. The churchyard was washed away in the serious flood of 1607 and services at St. Mary's ceased later that century.

Walk past the Great Western Hotel (9) on your left.

This is a superb example of High Victorian architecture, and also one of the best examples of random polygonal-jointed walling in Cardiff. The history of the hotel is a bit of a mystery - it was definitely built by 1879 and was probably in existence a few years earlier to cater for the growing number of rail travellers.

Near here was the South Gate. Outside the gate was the suburb of Soudrey, consisting of a single street called Shipman's Street. The South Gate was also known as the Ship Gate, and, because of the moorland which lay beyond the town wall, the Moorgate. This area of town grew in importance with the opening of the Glamorganshire Canal in 1794, and in 1802 the gate and part of the wall were removed for the construction of a new road. There is another blue plaque on the St. Mary Street side of the Great Western Hotel.

Cross over St. Mary Street by the Great Western Hotel. On your right, in the middle of the road, is a statue of the Second Marquis of Bute in Peer's robes.

When the Second Marquis of Bute died in 1848 this statue, known locally as 'The Monument', was sculpted by I. Evan Thomas. It was the first statue to be erected in Cardiff, and originally stood in front of the old Town Hall, in the middle of High Street. The statue was moved to its present position in 1879.

Walk straight on, along Mill Lane.

Here, the town wall followed the course of the western bank of the Glamorganshire Canal, which used to run alongside Mill Lane.

Cross The Hayes. On the left as you look down the Hayes is the cream Capel Tabernacl (10).

The name Hayes is thought to come from the Norman-French haie, and the Middle English heye, meaning 'an area of small enclosures and gardens'.

Capel Tabernacl is one of Cardiff's three Welsh-language chapels. Welsh Baptists have met here since 1821, though the existing building, designed by John Hartland in elegant Regency style, was rebuilt in just six months in 1865. A characteristic feature of many of the early non-conformist chapels in Wales was that the chapel was built above a school hall. This was done for

The Old Town Hall, showing the original site of the statue of the Second Marquis of Bute

two reasons: to economise on land, and to make the building as prominent as possible.

Continue straight on along Bridge Street until you come to the library. Turn left here onto St. David's Link. On the left is the Oxford Arcade (11).

Near here a watch tower, called Cock's Tower, stood on the bend of the town wall to guard the eastern approaches to the town. It was demolished in about 1860, after the canal boatmen complained that they had difficulty steering around it.

Walk to the end of St. David's Link. To your left, on Hill Street, are the South Wales Electricity Showrooms.

From Cock's Tower the wall ran through the site now occupied by these showrooms. This section of the wall was the last to be destroyed, in 1901.

If it is open, go into the St. David's Shopping Centre by the Hill

Street entrance. This walkway is called Town Wall because it follows the route of the wall. Turn left and walk along another walkway called St. David's Way.

A broad black line on the ground marks the route of the town wall.

The next part of the walk deviates from the route of the town wall to incorporate more places of historical interest.

Leave the St. David's Shopping Centre by the exit at the end of St. David's Way. This brings you onto Working Street, opposite the Old Library (12).

(If the shopping centre is closed, you can get to the Old Library from Hill Street by walking towards the statue of John Batchelor in the Hayes and turning right).

The Hayes site was selected for building the 'Cardiff Free Library, Museum, and Schools for Science and Art' in 1879. A competition was held for the design of the building and over a hundred plans were submitted anonymously, marked only with a motto. The winning one, called 'Reference', was the work of Seward and Thomas. Building began in 1880 and the Mayor (Mr. John McConnochie) laid the foundation stone on 27th October. Copies of local newspapers and the 'London Times' of that date, and a specimen of each coin for that year were placed within the cavity of the stone. When the building was finished in 1882 it was less than half its present size, reaching from St. John's churchyard to the tiled corridor. Being a multi-purpose building, the library soon proved far too small. In fact, the atmosphere in the overcrowded newspaper and magazine room was described as 'offensive and injurious to health'. The Schools for Science and Art were moved out and an extension was built between 1893 and 1896, designed by the same architects. This building housed Cardiff's Central Library until 1988 when the new library was built.

Turn left and walk to the last pillar on the left before St. David's Hall (13).

There is another blue plaque here, marking the site of the first gasworks in Cardiff. The gasworks, which opened in 1821, was situated near the Glamorganshire Canal so that coal could be unloaded easily. Cardiff Castle was one of the first buildings in the town to be lit by gas.

Turn right between the Old Library and the Hayes Island Snack Bar (14).

The Hayes Island Snack Bar was built in 1911 as the Tramway Parcel Express Office. From here couriers delivered parcels all over town. This closed in 1939 and the premises were converted to a snack bar just after the Second World War.

On your right is the imposing Hayes facade of the Old Library's extension. It is crowned with a bust of Pallas Athene, the goddess of wisdom, literature, and the arts, and her two owls. The arch below contains figures representing Literature, Calligraphy, and Printing. Above it, in Welsh, is the motto: 'Ni bydd doeth ni ddarlleno' (No wisdom without reading).

Take the first right onto Trinity Street.

On the right is the main Trinity Street entrance to the Old Library, flanked by two larger-than-life figures representing Study, and Rhetoric. These were sculpted by William Taylor who used his wife as the model. The square panels, carved by R.B. Boulton, represent (from the left): Agriculture, Manufacture,

Commerce, Culture (the only female figure), Music, and Architecture. The entrance to the Craft Centre Shop, to the left of the main entrance, leads down the tiled corridor. The tiles were manufactured by Maw and Co. of Shropshire, then the world's largest tileworks. The series of tiles depicting the four seasons, night, and morning were designed by Walter Crane.

Next to the Old Library is a public garden (15).

This site was part of St. John's churchyard and some old headstones remain.

On the left is Cardiff Central Market (16).

This was the site of gardens adjoining the old County Gaol until 1835, when the first St. Mary Street Market was built. This market was known as the New Market because it succeeded covered markets held in the Old Town Hall. The Market Tavern, next to the present market's Trinity Street entrance, was, until recently, called the New Market Tavern in memory of this. The population explosion in Cardiff in the nineteenth century led to serious overcrowding in the market, and in 1890 the New Market was demolished and the present Central Market built on the same site. This was opened in 1891 and a bronze plaque marking the occasion can be found by the stairs near the Trinity Street entrance. Many of the stallholders have traded in the Central Market for decades, and Marks and Spencer began their operations here with a Penny Bazaar, before moving to larger premises in Queen Street.

On the right, opposite the Market, is the church of St. John the Baptist (17).

Built within the town walls in about 1180, St. John's is the only surviving medieval building in central Cardiff, apart from the castle. St. John's was originally a chapel-of-ease to

St John's Church

Cardiff's first church, St. Mary's, serving, in particular, the population of the nearby castle. St. John's remained a dependent chapel, under the control of the monks of Tewkesbury Abbey, until the Reformation in the sixteenth century. When St. Mary's was badly damaged in the flood of 1607, St. John's became Cardiff's parish church.

After suffering damage in Owain Glyndwr's rebellion in 1404, St. John's was almost entirely rebuilt in Perpendicular style. The 132 feet high pinnacled 'Somerset' tower was built in 1473. It was commissioned by Lady Isobel Neville, daughter of Warwick 'The Kingmaker', and designed by John Hart. In the nineteenth century the church was enlarged to cater for the rapidly growing population.

There are many interesting features inside the church, which is open most days. The Lady Chapel on the north side of the chancel contains the Herbert monument, the Jacobean tomb of the Herbert brothers, John and William. The stained glass windows in this chapel commemorate the church's association with the castle - showing the heraldry of all the families connected with the castle since the Norman conquest.

Sometimes it is possible to take a guided tour up the tower, which houses the clock room and the peal of ten bells. The oldest bell dates from 1708, and the largest, the tenor bell, weighs twenty-seven hundredweight. The gallery, at the foot of the tower, was originally a musicians' gallery and used to house the organ, which is now located in the only remaining part of the original church. Near the gallery is one of George Pace's steel Crown chandeliers, reflecting the tracery on top of the tower. The positioning of this chandelier is unfortunate as there is no convenient place to lean a ladder. This means that scaffolding has to be erected below the light whenever a bulb needs changing!

Turn right after the church. On the corner is a pub, The Owain Glyndwr (18).

This pub stands on one of the oldest inn sites in Cardiff. The first inn on this site was the Mably Arms in 1731, and a later pub on this site was called the Tennis Court Inn, because an adjoining brewery had a tennis court in its yard.

Turn left, then take the first right onto Queen Street.

Queen Street used to be called Crockerton Street. It was the main thoroughfare through Crockherbtown, the suburb outside the East Gate, possibly so named because it was an area where herbs and pot (crock) vegetables were grown. Crockerton Street was controversially renamed in 1887 in honour of the Golden Jubilee of Queen Victoria. Crockherbtown Lane, a little lane off Park Place, nearly opposite the Park Hotel, is now the only reminder of this ancient district of Cardiff.

Walk along Queen Street until just before you reach The Friary (the first street on your left). Here we rejoin the route of the town wall as it emerges from the St. David's Shopping Centre.

This is where the East Gate stood, a fortified triple arched stone gateway with living quarters for the keeper. On the ground, blocks of black and red bricks, separated where the openings of the gate would have been, mark the site of the old wall. A blue plaque at the corner of the Friary tells how travellers on the ancient road between Gloucester and Swansea would have come through this gate. The gate was demolished in 1781 to improve the toll road.

When the Glamorganshire Canal was built, Crockherbtown lock stood by the site of the old gate. There was also a weighbridge here until 1894. Canal tolls were calculated on the basis of the weight of cargo and the distance travelled.

Walk along The Friary.

From Queen Street the wall continued northwards to a small watch tower on the site opposite the Job Centre. This tower collapsed in about 1842 because of nearby mining operations. At the tower the wall turned westwards, towards the castle.

Turn left at the end of the Friary and walk along Kingsway until you come to Northgate (the Lloyds Bank Information Centre), on the left (19).

This was the site of the North or Senghenydd Gate, the entrance from Caerphilly. Like the East Gate it was large enough to accommodate the keeper, who lodged in the upper storey. From here the wall joined the castle defences and a small part of it can still be seen across the road. This gate was demolished in 1787. There is another blue plaque on the wall of Northgate.

Cross the road and return to the castle to complete your walk. If you feel in need of refreshment there are many pleasant cafes and pubs nearby.

THE CIVIC CENTRE

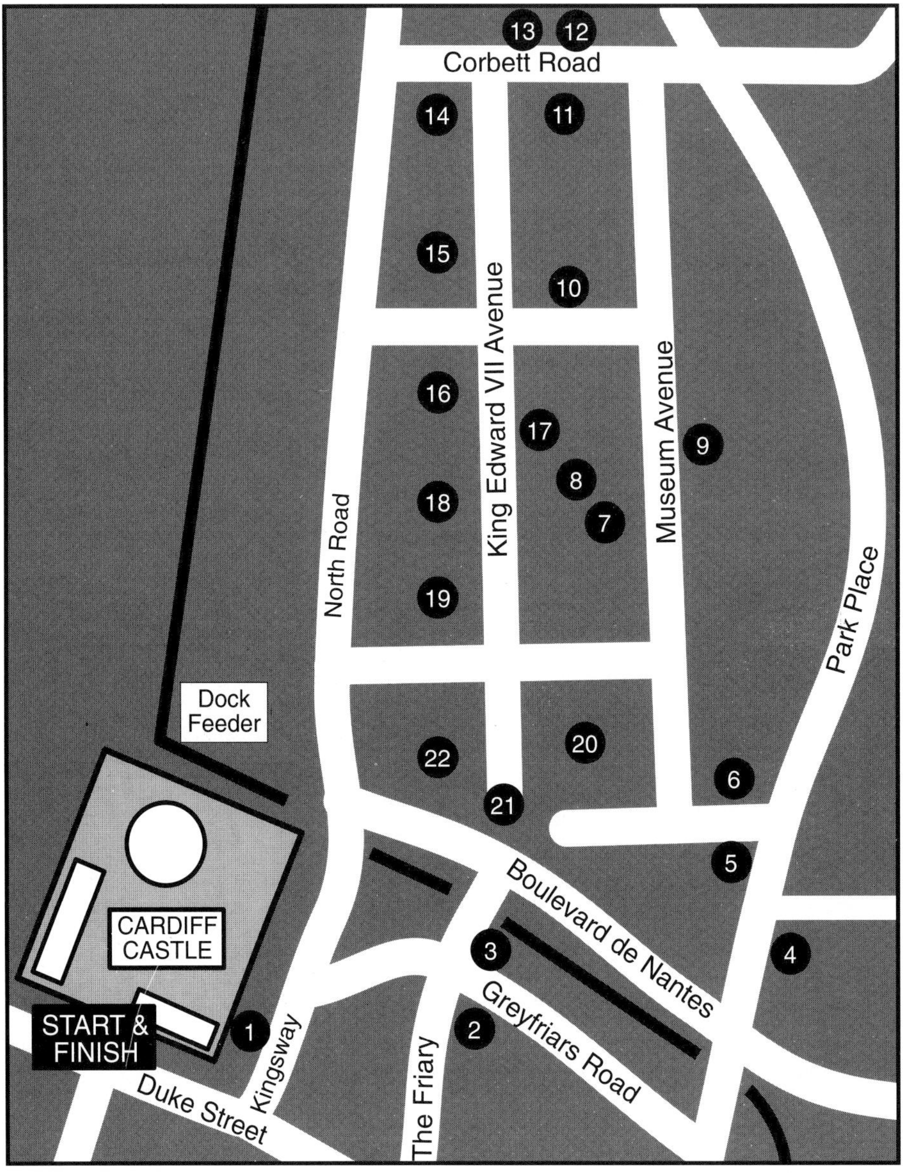

WALK 2
OS Sheet 171. 181 765 - 1.5 miles (2.4km)

THE CIVIC CENTRE

This walk is a circular walk, from Cardiff Castle, round the Civic Centre, acclaimed as one of the finest in Europe. The Civic Centre consists of a group of dignified public buildings, made from Portland stone (which comes from the Isle of Portland in Dorset), arranged around a small central park.

A History of the Civic Centre

The Civic Centre is situated in Cathays Park. The name Cathays is thought to originate from the words catt and hays, meaning 'a small enclosure'. The earliest form of the name is Cate Hayes, recorded in 1682, and thought to refer to garden allotments in the area. In the eighteenth century most of the land in Cathays consisted of two farms, Cathays, and Dobbin Pits. The latter farm probably takes its name from the fifteenth century daubing pits which were situated where Colum Road now stands. From these pits the townspeople would collect clay to daub onto their houses.

Much of the land at Cathays used to belong to the Herbert family, but by 1815 the Bute family had acquired it all and the area between Park Place and North Road was enclosed. This became known as Cathays Park.

In the mid-nineteenth century Cardiff experienced a population explosion and the Corporation negotiated to buy Cathays Park as a public open space. Negotiations were unsuccessful, but the Corporation approached Lord Bute again in 1892, this time with proposals to use Cathays Park for municipal buildings. Lord Bute offered to sell thirty-eight acres for £120,000, but some Council members opposed the idea, arguing that the site was too large, too expensive, and too restrictive. It was also opposed by the ratepayers of St. Mary Street who wanted to keep the town hall in the town centre. Several other sites were suggested - the Arms Park and Temperance Town - and so the 'Battle of the Sites' began.

Cathays Park was eventually chosen and in 1898 Lord Bute sold the whole fifty-nine acres for £161,000. There were certain conditions of sale which restricted the layout of roads, preserved the trees, and ensured that only public buildings were to be built in the Civic Centre.

Facing the main entrance to Cardiff Castle, turn right and follow the castle wall. When you come to the subway (1) go down the steps and turn right to go through it.

The Glamorganshire Canal used to run through this tunnel. A rubbing post for the rope which pulled the barges through the tunnel can still be seen on the corner of the underpass.

Turn left when you come out of the subway on the other side of the road, go up the steps, then turn right and follow the road round to the traffic lights by The Friary. The massive tower block on the right hand side of the road is the Pearl Assurance building (2). This is built on the site of the old Greyfriars friary.

In the thirteenth century a holy order inspired by St. Francis of Assisi was established. The Franciscan monks wore grey habits and became known as Greyfriars. In 1280 the Greyfriars founded their Cardiff friary, on land given to them by Gilbert de Clare, just outside the north wall of the town, near the north and east gates. The Greyfriars, denouncing all worldly wealth, devoted their lives to helping the poor and sick, which made them very popular with the local people. They were also sympathetic towards the Welsh, and Llywelyn Bren, the leader of the Welsh revolt in 1316, who was executed as a traitor in 1318, was buried in their church. It was largely because of this that the Greyfriars friary was spared in Owain Glyndwr's attack on Cardiff in 1404.

After the Reformation in 1538 the two friaries in Cardiff, Greyfriars and Blackfriars, were sold to Sir George Herbert of Swansea. His grandson, Sir William Herbert, built a mansion on the Greyfriars' site where the Herbert family lived until about 1730, after which time the house fell into disrepair.

In 1793 the Bute family bought the Greyfriars site from William Herbert and, in 1887, the Third Marquis of Bute excavated it. He uncovered a late thirteenth century church, containing about thirty graves, and found evidence of a hall, dormitory, kitchen, stable, and barn. Outside the church was a medieval burial ground.

In the late 1960s the remains of the picturesque ruin of Herbert House were removed when the Pearl Assurance building was built. Out of character with the rest of the city the tower block has few admirers. Now the only reminder of the Greyfriars is the street name 'Greyfriars Road'.

Cross the road at the pedestrian crossing then head towards the subway leading to the civic buildings. Turn right just before you get to the subway. There is a drinking fountain (3) on your right.

This drinking fountain was erected by William Alexander, Mayor of Cardiff, in 1860. The waterway beneath is the old dock feeder, built in 1834. The feeder drew water from the River Taff and carried it to the Bute West Dock, where it was used to flush away any mud brought in by the tide, and to maintain the water level.

Walk beside the dock feeder, under the trees, until you come to the pedestrian crossing at the end. Cross over the busy Boulevard de Nantes.

The name of this street is a reminder of one of the cities that Cardiff is twinned with, Nantes. To the east of Park Place, Boulevard de Nantes changes its name to Stuttgart Strasse - Stuttgart is another of Cardiff's twin cities.

Walk up Park Place.

This street contains some of the best Victorian Gothic architecture in Cardiff. These houses used to be the homes of wealthy families, but now most of the premises are offices or university buildings.

On the right is number 20, Park House (4).

This is the most striking of all the buildings on this road. Designed by William Burges (who renovated Cardiff Castle), it was built in 1874 for Mr. McConnochie, Mayor of Cardiff and Lord Bute's engineer for the Cardiff Docks. It is a Grade II listed building.

Just after Park House turn left into Gorsedd Gardens and follow the path round the Gorsedd Circle (5).

The standing stones in this circle are Triassic sandstone, a popular building material in Victorian Cardiff. They were erected for the Welsh National Eisteddfod held in Cardiff in 1899.

Leave Gorsedd Gardens opposite the National Museum of Wales (6).

Founded in 1907 by Royal Charter to house the national collection, the aim of the National Museum of Wales is: 'To teach the world about Wales, and the Welsh people about the land of their fathers'. An architectural competition was held for the design of the building in 1910 and the winners were Smith and Brewer. Their imposing, classical design blends in very well with the City Hall and the Law Courts. The foundation stone was laid in 1912, but work stopped during the First World War and it was not until 1927 that the building was officially opened by King George V. A Book of Remembrance for the Welshmen who died in the Second World War is kept here, next to Dylan Thomas's death mask. The museum has recently been extended and was granted a new Royal Charter by the Queen in 1990.

Park House

Walk along Museum Avenue, the road to the west of the museum. On your left, after City Hall (20), is a small park called Alexandra Gardens.

This beautifully laid out ornamental garden, covering nearly six acres, forms the heart of the Civic Centre and is a haven from the bustle of the city. It was named after Queen Alexandra and opened in 1910. The garden, which is surrounded by a beech hedge, contains many flowering cherry trees - spectacular in the springtime, formal seasonal beds, and rare and unusual trees and shrubs.

Take the first entrance into the park. The Spanish Civil War Monument (7) is to your right.

This monument is the latest addition to Alexandra Gardens, being erected in the autumn of 1992. It is dedicated to the Welsh Volunteers for liberty who defended democracy in the Spanish Civil War. The inscription in Welsh says: 'I goflo'r Cymry a aeth i Sbaen 1936-1938' (To remember the Welshmen who went to Spain). There are three quotes on the memorial, two in English and one in Welsh. The Welsh quotation by T.E. Nicholas, 'Dros ryddid daear', means 'For the freedom of the earth'.

Walk to the large monument in the centre of the Gardens. This is the Welsh National War Memorial (8).

Designed by J.N. Comper and unveiled in 1928, the Welsh National War Memorial commemorates the Welsh men and women who were killed in the First World War. On the frieze in English it says: 'Remember here in peace those who in tumult of war by sea, on land, in air, for us and for our victory, endureth unto death'. The more emotive Welsh inscription is: 'I feibion Cymru a roddes eu bywyd dros eu gwlad. Ger y ffos yn gorffwyso yn y nwyfre yn hofran yn rhyfel' (To the sons of Wales who gave their lives for their country. By the ditch resting, in the heavens hovering in war). In 1949 a dedication to the memory of those who died in the Second World War was added. This can be found on the angular part of the frieze, above you as you face the winged Messenger of Victory, and says: 'Dros for fe droes i farw' (Overseas they went to die). Facing the entrances are bronze statues of a soldier, a sailor, and an airman, lifting wreaths towards the Messenger of Victory, who is holding a cross-like sword. The statues were modelled by A.B. Pegram. Every second Sunday in November a remembrance service is held at this monument.

Turn right at the war memorial and leave the park by the side entrance opposite the University of Wales College, Cardiff's main building (9).

Welsh National War Memorial

The University College of South Wales and Monmouthshire, founded in 1883, was originally housed in the old Cardiff Infirmary building in Newport Road. The year after it was established the college was granted a Royal Charter, and in 1893 all the Welsh colleges became constituent members of the University of Wales. In 1903 it was decided to build a new college in Cathays Park, and the architect, Caroe, designed the building in an early English Renaissance style. The first section opened in 1909. After running into financial difficulties, University College, Cardiff merged with the University of Wales Institute of Science and Technology (UWIST) to form the University of Wales College, Cardiff (UWCC) in 1988. Today the university has 10,600 students.

The statue standing in Alexandra Gardens facing the main university building is of Henry Austin Bruce, the first president of the University College of South Wales and Monmouthshire.

Turn left and walk up Museum Avenue beside the Welsh Office (10) and (11).

The old building (10), facing Alexandra Gardens, was started in 1914, but wasn't finished until 1938 because work was suspended during the First World War. The building was originally used as offices for the Welsh Board of Health, but when Cardiff became the capital of Wales it was used as the headquarters of the Welsh Office. Designed by P.K. Hanton on simple classical lines, interesting features of the building are: a grey Welsh slate roof, heraldic shields bearing the Arms of the old counties and county boroughs of Wales on the window panels, and, above the main entrance, a stone carving of the Royal Coat of Arms.

A huge extension, the Crown Offices (11), designed by Alex Gordon and partners, was added to the back of the building in 1980 to make the building the largest in the Civic Centre. The extension is joined to the old building by an overhead walkway and has a four-storey car park beneath it. Rumours of a nuclear fallout shelter in the basement have been denied, but the building does have bombproof glass and even the net curtains are said to be bombproof and have to be specially cleaned.

Turn left at Corbett Road and walk around the back of the Welsh Office. About eighty yards on the right hand side is Aberdare Hall (12).

This may look like a set for a Hammer horror but in actual fact it is a women's hall of residence. Designed by Herbert Wills, it was built in 1893 as accommodation for forty-two female students and was notoriously strict. It has been extended several times and now houses 125 students, sixty-five percent of whom are in their first year at university.

Next to Aberdare Hall is the imposing entrance to Queen Anne Square (13).

This elegant collection of thirty Georgian style houses and a lodge, arranged around tree-lined lawns, was built on a site called the 'William Treat Field'. This was where annual treats were held for local children. The Square was the idea of the Marquis of Bute in the 1930s, and was designed, under his supervision, by Howard Williams. The Marquis was adamant that the Square should be exclusively private, and would not allow fences in the front gardens, only lawns separated by footpaths. Most Sundays the Marquis would stroll around the Square admiring its unique character. Construction of the entrance began in 1934 but, hampered by the Second World War, it was not until the early 1960s that the Square was completed.

The Square has had a chequered history. In the Second World War it was used as a parking spot for tanks, and in the 1970s it fell into disrepair because of threatened expansion of the university. However, the existing freehold residents have now bought the Square to ensure its survival.

Turn left at the end of the Welsh Office and walk down King Edward VII Avenue. On the right hand corner is the Redwood Building (14).

This building stands on the former site of the old Cathays farmhouse. Later, the first Marquis of Bute built a large mansion known as Cathays House on the site. This was demolished in 1815 by his grandson, the Second Marquis, who preferred to live at Cardiff Castle. The Redwood Building was formerly part of the Welsh College of Advanced Technology, which became UWIST. Designed by Percy Thomas and built in 1961, the Redwood is a fairly box-like building but has interesting statuary over the doors.

The next building on the right is the Temple of Peace and Health (15).

This is another of Percy Thomas's buildings, and was erected in 1938 as a gift to the Welsh nation by the first Lord Davies of Llandinam, to serve as a monument to the causes of peace and health. Fittingly, it is now occupied by South Glamorgan Health Authority and the Welsh Centre for International Affairs. Behind the massive columns are three large windows fitted with bronze grilles, above which are figures representing Health, Justice, and Peace. Built in the form of a letter T, the temple is situated in the centre portion. The temple, which is used as a venue for cultural and social organisations, is lined with dove-grey marble, symbolising the emblem of peace. To emphasise the international nature of the building, materials used in its construction came from all over the world.

Beneath the temple is a crypt where a Book of Remembrance, containing the beautifully handwritten names of 35,000 Welshmen who died in the First World War, is kept. The book has 1,100 vellum pages and a page is turned every day at 11am. As most of the men died on Belgian or French soil the book is encased in glass and French bronze, and supported by a pedestal of Belgian marble. It is possible to go and see the crypt between 9am and 5pm on weekdays and is well worth a visit. Seeing the massive book crammed with names really highlights the tragedy of the First World War - indeed of any war.

In the reception area of the Temple of Peace is a Japanese Peace Column, delivered by a delegation from the World Peace Movement of Japan in 1982. It carries the message 'May peace prevail on Earth' in four languages.

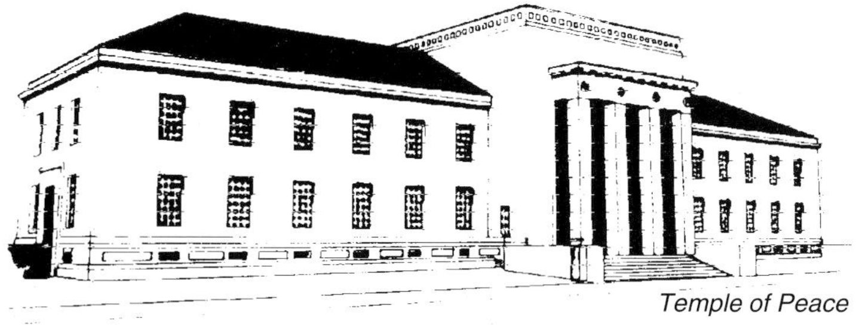

Temple of Peace

Next to the Temple of Peace is the Bute Building (16).

Before the First World War an architectural competition was held for the design of a new Technical College. The winners were Jones and Thomas and the resulting Bute Building was Percy Thomas's first major building project. Opened in 1916 the Bute Building was the only building in the Civic Centre to be completed during the First World War. In 1957 the Technical College became a College of Advanced Technology, and in 1967 it became a constituent college of the University of Wales, UWIST. The Bute Building now houses several of the University's libraries. The eye-catching red dragon above the entrance was made by a Welsh blacksmith and hoisted up to its present position in 1985.

Go back into Alexandra Park via the side entrance opposite the Bute Building. Turn right and then take a small paved path to the left which leads to the Falklands Memorial (17).

This is a garden within a garden, at the centre of which is a large stone bearing a plaque in memory of the six men from Cardiff who were killed in the Falkland Islands campaign of 1982. A blue cedar tree has been planted for each of the men and the grass growing between the paving stones is deliberately left to symbolize the terrain of the Falklands.

Go out of the park by the next entrance on the right, opposite the Mid Glamorgan County Hall (18).

This building, designed by Harris and Moodie, was opened in 1912 as the centre of administration for Glamorgan County Council, formed after the County Councils Act of 1888. The larger-than-life statuary on either side, designed by Albert Hodge, symbolise mining, and the sea (navigation), the main sources of income at the time. In 1974 local government reorganisation led to the old county of Glamorgan being subdivided into Mid, South, and West Glamorgan. Although the County Hall is in South Glamorgan, it was made the headquarters of the Mid Glamorgan County Council.

The next building on the right hand side is the University Registry (19).

This attractive two-storey building, designed by Wills and Anderson in the Renaissance style, is the administrative headquarters for the University of Wales. It was built in 1903 and was the first building to be erected on the Cathays Park site. The chain posts outside are topped with sleeping dragons.

Falklands Memorial

City Hall (20) is the next building on the left, walk round to the front (south side) of the building.

City Hall was designed in an English Renaissance style by the architects Lancaster, Stewart, and Rickards of London. The foundation stone was laid in 1901, when it was destined to be a Town Hall. However, by the time the building was finished in 1906, Cardiff had been granted the status of a city and the building became the City Hall. A large two-storey building with square pavillions at each of the four corners, its most eye-catching features are the fiery Welsh Dragon made of lead which tops the dome of the council chamber, and the 194 feet high clock tower. The figures on the four corners of the tower, just below the clock, represent the four winds and were modelled by H.C. Fehr, who also modelled the dragon. Surrounding the main window of the council chamber, above the portico, is statuary depicting the sea receiving the Severn and the three local rivers - the Taff, Ely, and Rhymney.

The ornamental pool in front of City Hall was completed in 1969 to commemorate the investiture of Prince Charles as Prince of Wales. The fountains are in the shape of a fleur-de-lis.

City Hall is open to the public between 8am and 5pm on weekdays. A free leaflet available from the reception desk gives details of what there is to see inside. This includes: another Book of Remembrance (for those who died serving with the Merchant Navy in the First World War); the Marble Hall, where marble statues of 'The Heroes of Wales', and the Corporation maces can be found; the Assembly Room, used as a public venue; and the Council Chamber, where the City Council meet once a month.

Between the Law Courts (22) and the City Hall is the South Africa War Memorial (21).

This is the work of Albert Toft. Erected by public subscription, it is a memorial to nearly 200 Welshmen who died in South Africa from 1899 to 1902. Bronze plaques bear the names of the main victories in which the Welsh regiments took part and the three figures represent Warfare and Courage, Grief, and Peace.

Opposite City Hall are the Law Courts (22).

The Law Courts, completed in 1906, were skilfully designed by Lancaster, Stewart, and Rickards, to be in harmony with City Hall but more austere. To enhance the feeling of unity between the buildings there are sculptures at the front of the buildings, reflecting the themes: 'Science and Education', and 'Commerce and Industry' on the Law Courts; and 'Poetry and Music', and 'Welsh Unity and Patriotism' on City Hall. In the Law Courts there are eight criminal courts and two chancery courts.

Go under the subway in front of the Law Courts to return to the castle and complete your walk. There are many pleasant cafes and pubs in the city if you feel in need of refreshment.

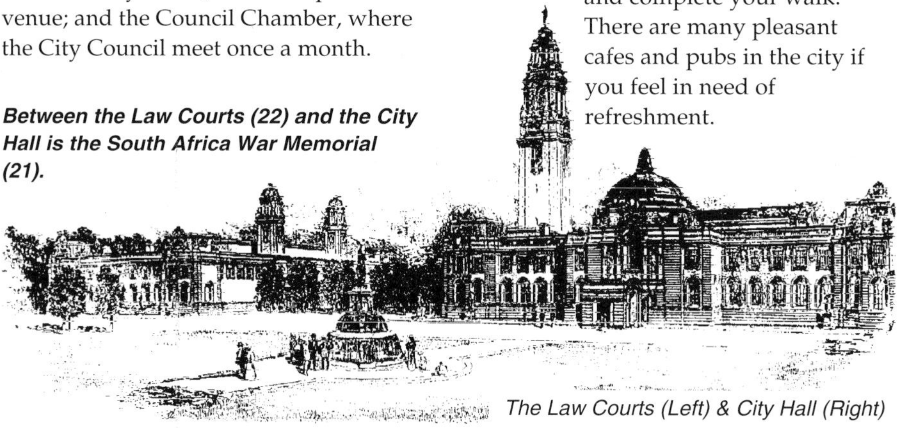

The Law Courts (Left) & City Hall (Right)

WALK 3 OS Sheet 171. 180 765
Circular 5.5 miles (8.8km);
linear 3 miles (4.8km)

CARDIFF CASTLE TO LLANDAFF CATHEDRAL

This walk begins by Cardiff Castle in the magnificent Bute Park. This was the private domain of the Bute family until 1947 when the Fifth Marquis granted Cardiff Castle and 146 acres of land in Bute Park to the people of Cardiff. Bute Park now extends from the shopping centre to Western Avenue, covering an area of over 350 acres, the largest expanse of parkland in the heart of any city outside London. The route continues beside the River Taff to Llandaff. Although Llandaff became part of Cardiff in 1922, it still retains a village atmosphere. Some of the features that help to give Llandaff its unique character can be seen on a short walk through the older part of the village, near the village green.

History of Llandaff and Llandaff Cathedral

Llandaff is situated beside a crossing point of the River Taff, near a Roman road and a prehistoric trackway. Because of this good communications network Llandaff became an important town. It was originally a lordship and a chartered borough, with its own market and fair. Built on a rocky escarpment above the alluvial plain of the River Taff, and on the border of the fertile Vale of Glamorgan, Llandaff was a self-supporting agricultural community with abundant market-gardens. However, in the nineteenth century, as a result of Cardiff's commercial success and phenomenal growth, Llandaff's rural nature changed as it became a much sought after residential area.

The name Llandaff means 'sacred enclosure near the Taff', and Llandaff Cathedral is built on one of the oldest church sites in Britain. St. Teilo reputedly established a monastery here, in a hollow on the banks of the River Taff, in the sixth century. Although nothing remains of this early monastery, pre-Christian burials from the Roman era have been discovered under the cathedral. Also, a tenth century wheel-headed cross, now in the south presbytery aisle, was discovered in the garden of the Bishop's Palace.

The cathedral has a long and chequered history. When Urban became Bishop of Llandaff in 1107 the church at Llandaff was a very simple affair. Bishop Urban decided to build a more impressive structure, and work on the first Norman cathedral began in 1120. Parts of this Norman cathedral can still be seen in the arches in the presbytery and choir aisles. In 1170 the nave was extended and the church largely rebuilt. North and south aisles were added in the thirteenth century.

In 1485 the Perpendicular, 105 feet high, Jasper Tower was added. This is said to have been commissioned by Jasper Tudor when he became Lord of Cardiff Castle after his victory at the Battle of Bosworth. During the Reformation and Civil War the cathedral was used as, amongst other things, an alehouse, and an animal shelter. By the eighteenth century it was derelict.

In 1734 John Wood from Bath built a controversial classical-style Italian temple within the ruins, but this was demolished in the nineteenth century when John Prichard rebuilt the cathedral. Prichard reconstructed the nave and added the 195 feet high Prichard Tower. On the north and south walls of the Cathedral he added sculptured heads of British monarchs from Richard III. Interestingly, he included the head of Oliver Cromwell. The cathedral suffered bomb damage in the Second World War and was rebuilt by George Pace between 1949 and 1960, when the David Chapel was added.

The interior of the cathedral has many interesting features. The most eye-catching is Sir Jacob Epstein's aluminium sculpture, 'Christ in Majesty', which was specially commissioned for Llandaff after the bombing. The figure, mounted on a cylindrical organ-case, weighs seven hundredweight and is fifteen feet high. There are many works of Pre-Raphaelite art in the cathedral, the most notable being Rossetti's altarpiece, 'The Seed of David', now found in St. Illtyd's Chapel.

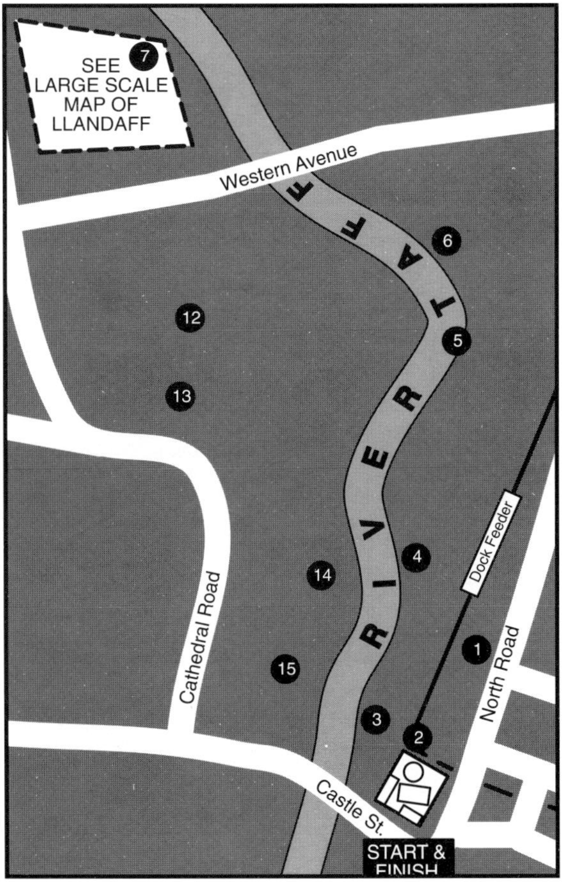

Facing the main entrance to Cardiff Castle, turn right and walk beside the castle wall, away from town. Continue until you come to a sign pointing through the car park on your left to the St. John's Ambulance Brigade Headquarters, and Cardiff Lawn Tennis Club. Go into Bute Park by this entrance. On your right are the Castle Mews (1). It is possible to go into the courtyard and look at the architecture.

These stables were designed for the Marquis of Bute by William Burges (who renovated Cardiff Castle), and built in two stages between 1869 and 1875. The Mews held twelve carriages, twenty-four horses, and housed up to twelve grooms. Even though it is quite a plain building, the gables, pointed arches, and timber balcony add interest and give it the Burges trademark. Today the building is used as offices and flats.

When you come out of the Mews, walk straight on towards the castle, past the tennis courts on the left. Turn right at the path junction and go over the bridge which crosses the dock feeder (2).

The dock feeder, built in 1834, drew water from the River Taff and carried it to the docks. Here it was used to flush out any mud brought in by the tide, and to maintain the water level.

Follow the path. On the right are the ruins of the Blackfriars friary (3).

In the thirteenth century a holy order inspired by St. Dominic was established. The Dominican monks wore black habits and became known as the Blackfriars. Arriving in Cardiff in 1242, the Blackfriars established their friary on land given to them by Richard de Clare. They were educated men who spent their time worshipping, and were not as popular as the Greyfriars, who devoted their time to helping the poor and sick. In 1404, Blackfriars, along with most of Cardiff, was burnt down by Owain Glyndwr, but it was rebuilt and used until the Reformation in 1538 when the friaries were abolished. Sir George Herbert bought the Cardiff friaries after the Reformation, but they fell into disrepair and gradually disappeared, probably to provide building materials for work at Cardiff Castle, which was also owned by the Herberts at the time.

In 1887 the Marquis of Bute excavated the site, uncovering the foundations of an Early English church, and fragments of other buildings including a dormitory, refectory, and infirmary. The cloisters where the monks walked silently every day, and the tomb of John Eaglescliffe, a Dominican Bishop of Llandaff who died in 1346, can still be seen.

Carry straight on where the path branches and follow it round to the right beside the River Taff. Continue until you come to an unusual sundial (4) on your right, just before the brick wall surrounding the nursery.

This sundial was designed by David Pettitt, who won the First International Festival of Iron design competition in 1989. There are 120 flowers incorporated into the design, which were made by blacksmiths from all over the world. The opening ceremony for the sundial, which tells the time for Cardiff and Xiamen, Cardiff's twin city in China, was on 10th May 1990.

Take the first small path on the left, after the sundial. This woodland path beside the river leads you to a weir (5).

The concrete construction in the middle of the weir is a salmon run.

Go through the gate near the suspension bridge and follow the path straight ahead, past the house on your right (6).

This is a nineteenth century Park Keeper's Lodge, built in the distinctive style of most of the Bute family's property.

Continue beside the river until you come to a road bridge over it. Go under the bridge and up the steps on the other side. At the road turn right, cross the river, then resume your walk on the other bank of the river.

The area of Cardiff across the river is called Gabalfa. This is derived from the Welsh word ceubalfa, meaning 'the place of the ferryboat'.

Take the first path on the left, towards the Cathedral (7).

This is an ancient avenue crossing the herb meadow of Arles Field.

Go through the kissing gate and walk up the hill, past the white Prebendal House on your left.

This seventeenth century house was one of six within the Cathedral Close which housed canons. At the beginning of the eighteenth century it was rebuilt and converted into an audit house. Now it is used for meetings, as a vestry, and

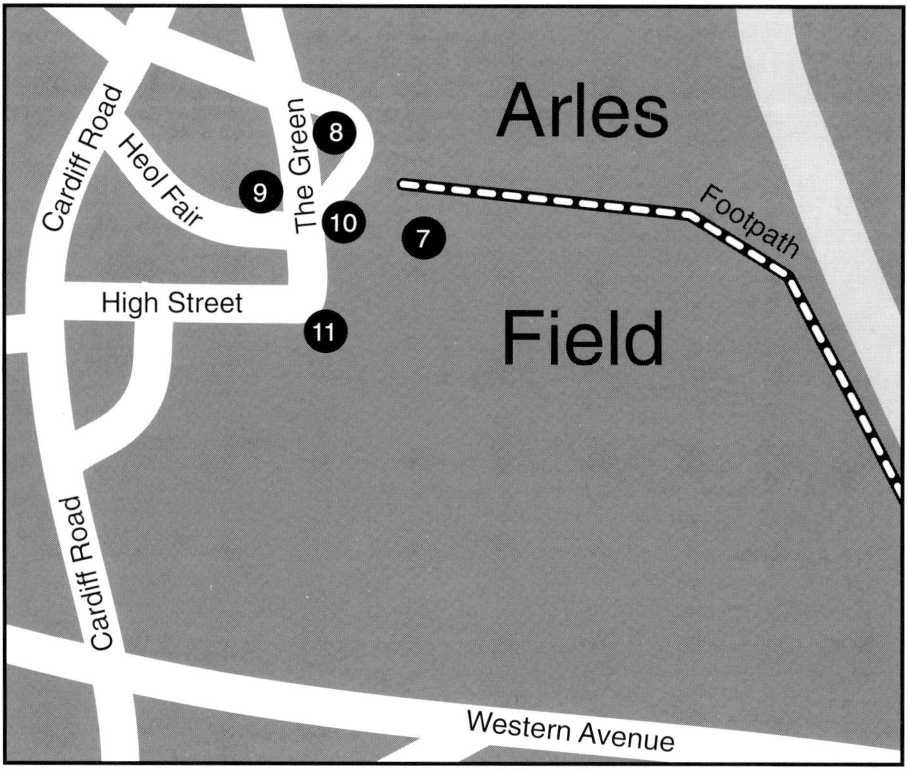

by the cathedral choir. The classical urns outide the entrance were part of the Italian temple, built within the ruins of the cathedral in the eighteenth century by John Wood.

Llandaff Cathedral (7) is the next building and takes you rather by surprise approaching it from this direction.

The graveyard surrounding the Cathedral is Victorian and several Llandaff bishops are buried here. The concave shape of the ground is due to an air raid which damaged the Cathedral in 1941.

After visiting the cathedral go up the Dean's Steps opposite the west door. At the top of these steps is the Llandaff War Memorial (8) and The Green.

The war memorial is a bronze sculpture of a mother, with a soldier on one side and a boy on the other. Designed by Sir William Goscombe John of Llandaff, it commemorates the men and women of the village, and old boys of the Cathedral School, who were killed in the two world wars. It has recently been refurbished.

The village green used to be an open space where markets and fairs were held. It was enclosed in 1897.

Walk around The Green and turn left at the road. On your right a little way ahead is a memorial to James Rice Buckley (9).

Buckley was the vicar of Llandaff for forty-six years and Archdeacon from 1913 to 1924. This memorial was also sculpted by Sir William Goscombe John.

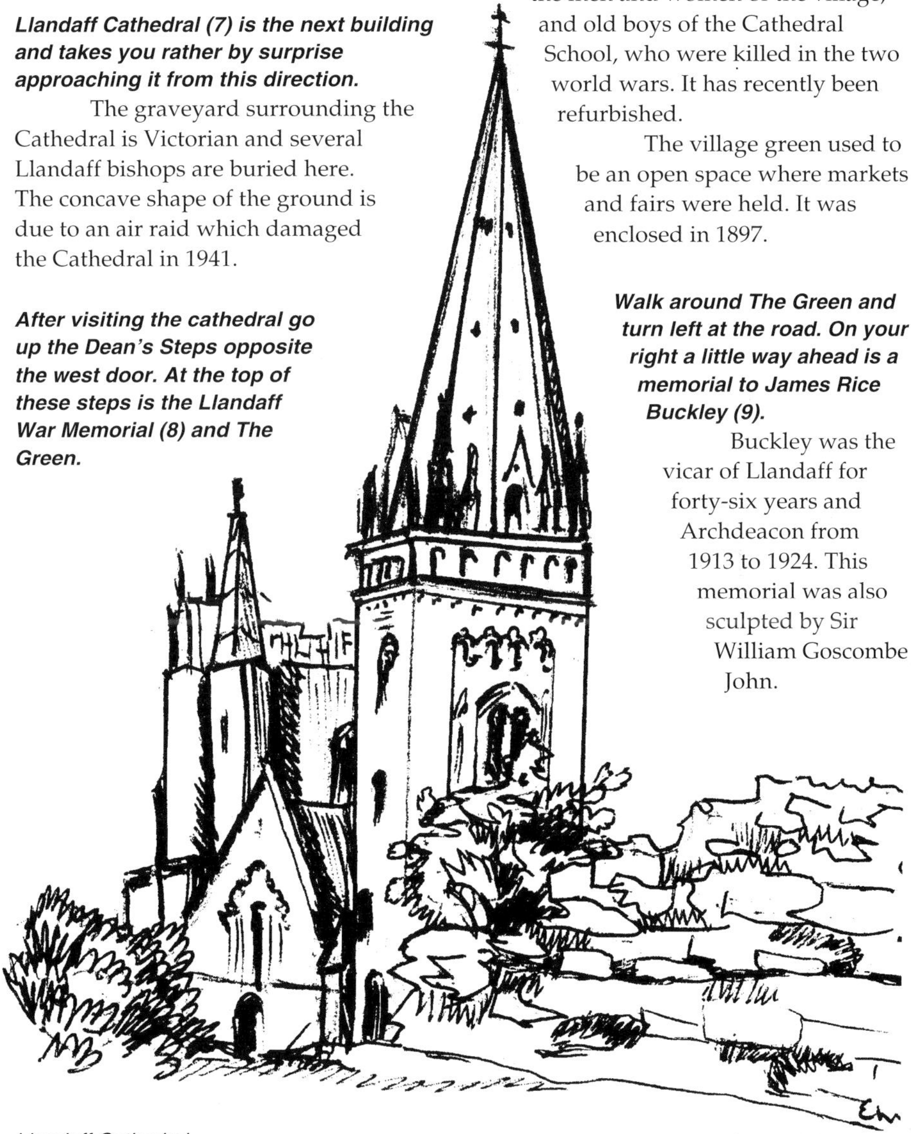

Llandaff Cathedral

Opposite this statue are the ruins of a bell tower.

This thirteenth century bell tower once held one of the largest bells in Britain, the five and a half ton 'Great Peter'. In 1488 'Great Peter' was exchanged for five smaller bells from Exeter, which were hung in the cathedral's Jasper Tower. The bell tower was ruined in the fifteenth century and the ruins were later enclosed by the Red Lion Inn, which was built on the site. In 1924 the Red Lion was demolished and the site was taken over by the City of Cardiff.

In front of the tower is the preaching cross (10).

Near here in 1188, Archbishop Baldwin of Canterbury and his chaplain, Giraldus Cambrensis, urged the Welsh, English, and Norman-French to join the Third Crusade - an event related by Gerald of Wales in his 'Journey through Wales'. The shaft dates back to the thirteenth century and the cross was restored in the nineteenth century.

Straight on, through the arch, is the Bishop's Palace (11).

There is some evidence to suggest that the earliest building on this site was erected in the late twelfth century. The present Bishop's Palace was built in the thirteenth century, although by whom it is not certain. Some believe it was built by William de Brewsa, who was Bishop from 1266 to 1287, whilst others think it was the work of Gilbert de Clare. Certainly the gatehouse of the Bishop's Palace shows similar features to parts of Caerphilly Castle, which was built by Gilbert de Clare. Also, the Bishop's Palace was strategically built near an important crossing point on the River Taff.

The Bishop's Palace was the main residence of the Bishops of Llandaff until the early fifteenth century when it was destroyed by Owain Glyndwr. After this the site was abandoned in favour of Mathern Palace near Chepstow and the ruins became a wilderness. On the wall to the left of the entrance, the roof-line of the Bush Inn, which ajoined the gatehouse in the eighteenth century, can be seen. In 1972 the walls, turrets, and gateway were restored and the courtyard made into a peaceful public garden.

If you feel in need of refreshment before you start the return journey, or if you want to catch a bus back to Cardiff, turn left when you come out of the Bishop's Palace and walk down the High Street. A little further, on your right, is the first of three nearby pubs, The Butcher's Arms. At the far end of the High Street on the left is The Black Lion, and on Cardiff Road, opposite the end of High Street, is The Maltsters Arms. Turn right at Cardiff Road and the bus stop is on your right hand side.

If walking back to Cardiff, make your way back to the Cathedral and walk down the hill past the Prebendal House again. Walk straight on, through the kissing gate, across Arles field, and back to the footpath beside the river. Turn right and follow the path. Cross the main road but keep the river on your left and walk back along the other bank of the Taff.
This takes you past the Equestrian Centre (12), Pontcanna fields (13), Glamorgan County Cricket Ground (14), and Sophia Gardens (15), to Castle Street. Turn left and cross the river. Cardiff Castle is on your left hand side.

WALK 4 OS Sheet 171. 135 804
Circular 4.75 miles (7.6km);
linear 2.5 miles (4.0km)

RADYR TO CASTELL COCH AND BACK VIA THE GLAMORGANSHIRE CANAL NATURE RESERVE

This walk begins from the railway station at Radyr and leads you beside the River Taff to Castell Coch, the fairytale Red Castle perched high on a wooded hillside near Tongwynlais. The route back includes the Glamorganshire Canal Nature Reserve, the last remaining stretch of the canal that helped to make Cardiff the thriving city that it is today.

History of the Glamorganshire Canal

Between 1750 and 1800 metal production in the towns north of Cardiff increased and by the nineteenth century Merthyr had become the largest town in Wales and the 'Iron Capital' of the world. In the early days, iron was transported by mule across the mountains to the quay at Cardiff. Then, in 1767, a road was built along the valley from Merthyr which meant that up to two tons of iron could be transported by horse-drawn wagons. As iron production increased, this form of transport became unviable and another alternative was sought - a canal was the obvious solution.

In 1790 a Bill was passed in Parliament authorising the construction of the Glamorganshire Canal, and in 1794 the main part of the canal was opened. Four years later the canal was extended to the sea-lock at the mouth of the river. More than fifty locks were required between Merthyr and Cardiff to control the water through a land fall of over 550 feet - a remarkable feat of engineering. Quarter mile markers were erected along the route to fix the position of wharves, landing places, stations, and sidings so that proprietors and traders could assess the mileage and tonnage rates.

Barges, carrying up to twenty-four tons of cargo, navigated the canal twenty-four hours a day, seven days a week. In 1838 over 320,000 tons of freight were transported along the canal. However, as trade continued to increase, the volume of traffic and number of locks caused delay. On average, the twenty-five mile journey took twelve hours.

For sixty years the canal prospered, but competition from the first Bute Dock, which opened in 1839, and the Taff Vale Railway, which opened in 1841, meant that by 1890 the canal was no longer making a profit. In 1915 the canal north of Pontypridd was closed and the last section, from Pontypridd to Cardiff, was closed in 1942. The only part of the Glamorganshire Canal still remaining is a half-mile stretch which has been preserved in the Glamorganshire Canal Nature Reserve.

Catch one of the frequent trains from Cardiff Central Station to Radyr. The walk begins at Radyr railway station.

RADYR TO
CASTELL COCH AND BACK

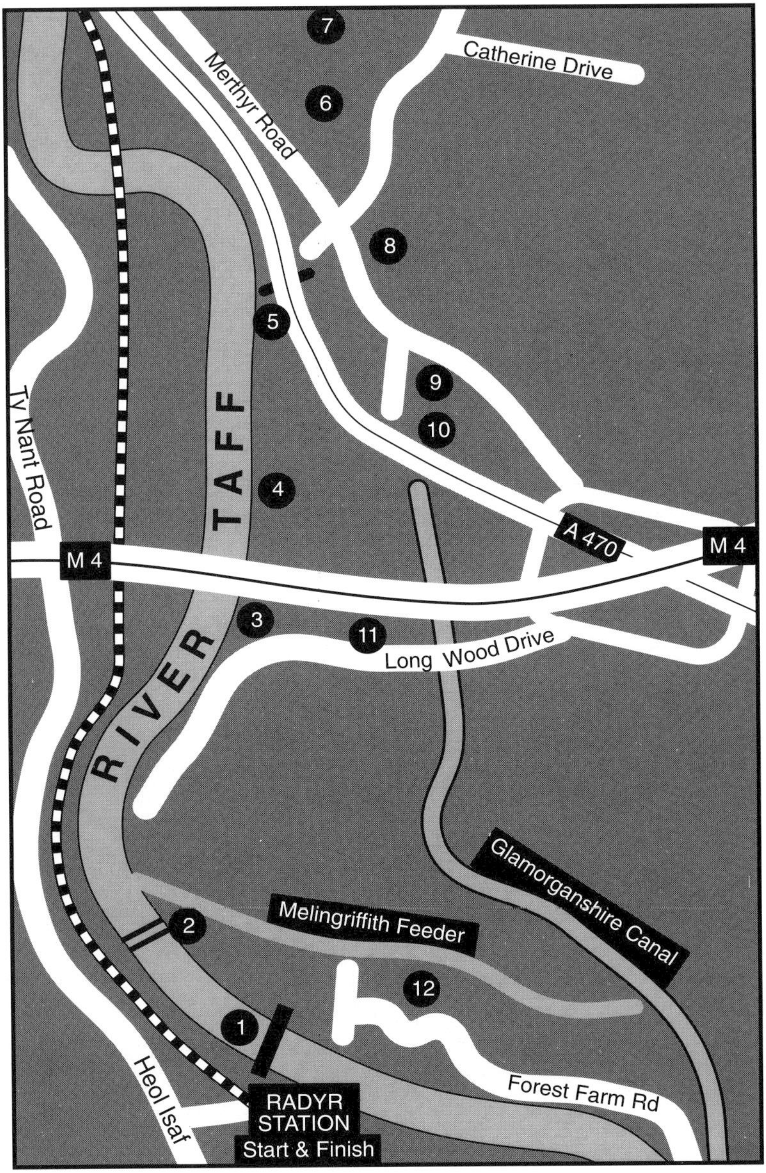

Take the path beside the station which leads you under the railway line and over a blue bridge (1) across the River Taff. Walk beside the river, following signs to Castell Coch, past the weir (2) and an old sluice gate.

At the path junction turn left, following the signs to Castell Coch (don't go down the path signed with the horse). Go past the seat in the corner (3), which is situated under 275,000 volts of electricity and within a stone's throw of the M4 (what a peaceful location for a seat!), and go under the M4.

Follow the path, through the squeeze stile, and go straight on, through the green gate (4). This path is part of the Taff Valley Heritage Trail and follows the river, through several kissing gates, to a white-washed house (5).

Go under the subway and left at the road on the other side. At the crossroads go straight on and continue, past the Lewis Arms, up the hill. On the left is Castle Farm (6).

From 1877 to 1923 the Third and Fourth Marquises of Bute experimented with growing vines in the fields north of this farm, with some commercial success.

Go past the golf course on your left and near the top of the hill, opposite Catherine Drive, turn left and walk down the driveway leading to Castell Coch (7).

Castell Coch was built by Gilbert de Clare in the thirteenth century to guard the entrance to the Taff. It occupies the site of an earlier Welsh stronghold built in the middle of the twelfth century by Ifor ap Meurig, Lord of Senghenydd.

Destroyed in the fifteenth century, Castell Coch was left as a ruin until the Third Marquis of Bute acquired it in the nineteenth century. He commissioned his friend William Burges to rebuild the castle and work began in 1875. It was completed in 1891, ten years after Burges's death. The exterior, apart from the circular towers topped by conical turrets which give a romantic appearance, is a sober reconstruction of a medieval castle. Burges even included a working drawbridge and portcullis at the entrance leading into the small courtyard. The interior, however, is richly decorated in the High Victorian fashion. The castle was designed for occasional occupation as there is no guest accommodation. In fact, the castle was hardly ever used, except to quarantine Bute's children when they were suffering from infectious diseases.

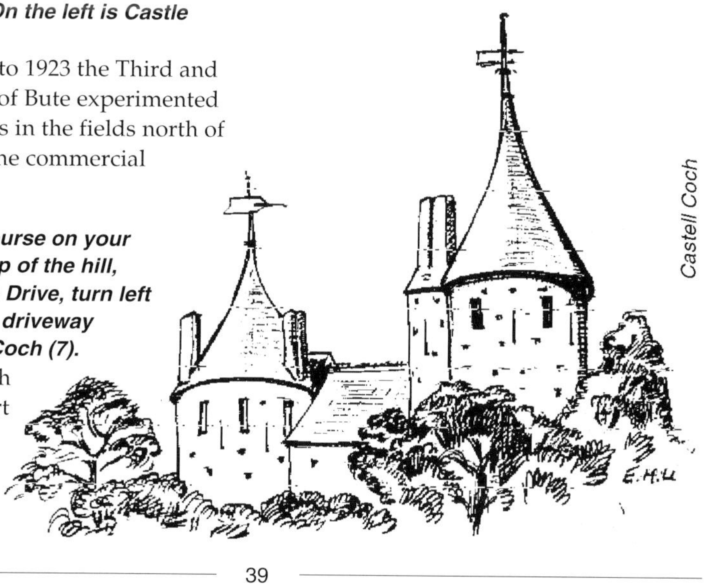

Castell Coch

In the twentieth century the Bute family gave Castell Coch to the local community. It is now a Grade I listed building, an ancient monument.

After visiting the castle, retrace your steps to the bottom of the hill. Liquid refreshment is available from the Lewis Arms (Brains) on your right, or, if you turn left and walk a little way along the main street, from the Old Ton Inn (Whitbread). If you want to catch a bus back to Cardiff there is a bus stop outside the church on your left hand side (8).

If walking back to Cardiff, continue along the main street, past the school on the right, to the last big house on the right hand side (9). Take the signed footpath to the left of this house, (access to it is part way up the drive), through a field. Keep to the hedge on the right hand side and join the path near the road. Go down the steps to the road and turn left. Then go under the bridge (10) and turn right at the junction, following the Cardiff cycle path signs.

Follow the road until you come to a footpath over the Taff. Don't go over this but turn left on the footpath. This path takes you back to the seat under the electricity pylon. Follow the path straight on then take the path to the left before you get to Amersham International.

The Amersham International Laboratories, designed by the Percy Thomas Partnership, have received many architectural awards. These include two Design Awards from the Royal Institute of British Architects (1982 & 1990), the Financial Times Architecture at Work Award (1982), the Concrete Society Commendation (1981), and the Gold Award from the Design Council of the National Eisteddfod of Wales. The fifty metre vertical stacks that tower over the thirty acre site are not chimneys, but ventilation shafts.

This area is rich in plant life, including several species of orchids.

When you get to a road (11) cross over it and rejoin the path on the other side. Turn left and follow the path, over a wooden stile, to the canal. Turn right and walk beside the canal on the old towpath.

The section of the canal within the Reserve was transferred to the City Council in 1944, and since 1967 the canal and adjacent woodland have been managed as a Nature Reserve. The area contains a variety of different habitat types and is rich in plant and animal life. Approximately a hundred species of birds have been seen at the reserve.

Follow the canal to the end and turn right at the road. Follow the cycle signs to Forest Farm (12).

Forest Farmhouse is an eighteenth century Grade II listed building restored by the British Trust for Conservation Volunteers as a regional headquarters. There is a short nature trail across the road if you have time for a little detour.

Follow the road until you reach the allotments then turn left. At the end of this path turn left again and cross the bridge to return to the train station.

If you have time to spare before your return train journey to Cardiff there is a pub nearby. To reach it, turn right outside the train station and go up Station Road. The Radyr Arms (Whitbread) is on your right hand side.

WALK 5 OS Sheet 171. 191 751
1.75 miles (2.8 km)

BUTETOWN AND THE DOCKS

This is a short tour around the area that made Cardiff the greatest coal port in the world. The walk first leads you through Mount Stuart Square, planned by the Marquis of Bute as a residential Square for professional people, which later became the commercial heart of Butetown. The route then continues to the inner harbour to look at the area near the docks.

History of Butetown and the Docks

Cardiff was historically divided into two parishes, St. John the Baptist and St. Mary's. Most of the southern parish, St. Mary's, which occupied 700 acres on the coast of the Bristol Channel, was marshy, grazing land known as 'The Moors'. The Glamorganshire Canal was the first intrusion into this area in 1798, and wharves and associated industries developed along its banks.

Much of the land in St. Mary's Parish was owned by the Bute family. In the 1820s the Second Marquis of Bute, realising that the canal was inadequate to deal with the transportation demands placed upon it, decided to risk his fortune to build a dock and develop the surrounding area. There were four main aspects to his plan: to build a main road from the centre of town to the foreshore; to build the dock; to construct a railway from Merthyr to Cardiff; and to lease land in the area for development. The road, Bute Street, was constructed in a straight line from The Hayes in 1830, and houses were built along it to house the dockworkers. With the opening of the first dock at Cardiff, the nineteen and a half acre Bute West Dock, in 1839, and the Taff Vale Railway linking Merthyr to Cardiff, in 1841, the coal industry became well established.

Within a decade the Bute West Dock was handling over a quarter of a million tons of coal per year. By 1855, the first year that coal from the Rhondda was exported, and the year that coal exports from Cardiff exceeded one million tons, it had become obvious that another dock was necessary. The Second Marquis of Bute had died in 1848 leaving a baby son, so the decision to build the second dock was taken by the trustees to his estate. The Bute East Dock, which opened in 1859, was capable of handling larger vessels, and by the end of that year the two docks were handling two million tons of cargo per year. Eighty percent of this trade was coal.

By 1860 Butetown was virtually complete, occupying a narrow area of land between Bute Street and the Glamorganshire Canal. The Marquis of Bute had conceived Butetown as a residential area for a wide social mix, and for a while this objective was achieved. The area, which became known as 'Tiger Bay' in the 1860s, attracted people of all races and social standing and became a cosmopolitan society, unique in Britain at that time. However, within a generation the professional people moved out to new, quieter suburbs, leaving Butetown to become a working class community, most of whom were connected with the

BUTETOWN AND THE DOCKS

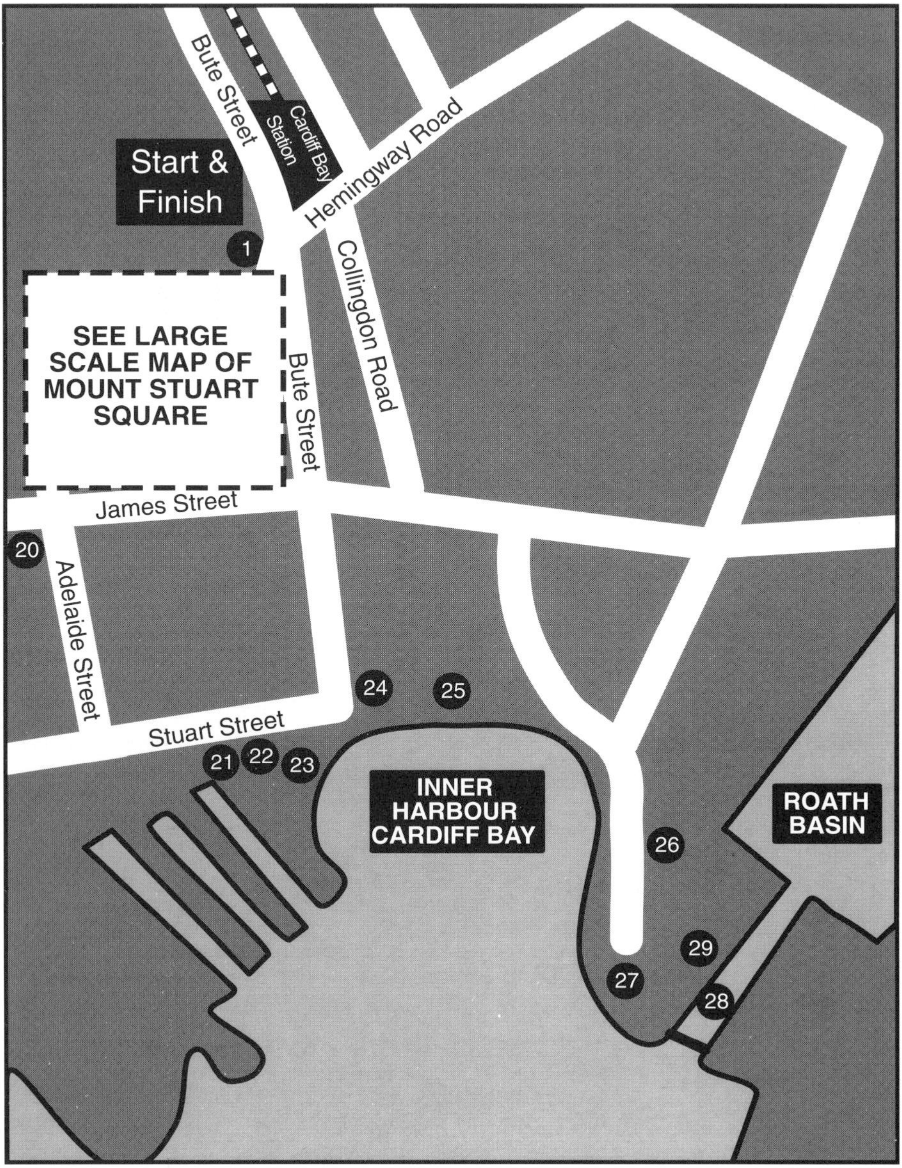

docks. The character of Butetown gradually changed from residential to commercial as houses were replaced by offices. The centre of the commercial activity became Mount Stuart Square, where the Coal and Shipping Exchange was opened in 1886.

Exports of coal continued to rise and another dock, the Roath Basin, was constructed in 1874. This did little to ease the situation and in 1887 the Roath Dock was built. Over thirty ship-repair yards and engineering works were also established, making Cardiff one of the primary ship-repair ports in the world. The last dock, the fifty-two acre Queen Alexandra Dock, opened in 1907. This was the largest masonry dock in the world at that time, capable of handling any vessel.

The peak of the coal exports from Cardiff came in 1913, when ten and a half million tons were exported, but this euphoric period did not last. Coal exports slumped after the First World War because of the dislocation and loss of markets and the more widespread use of oil. The docks became busy again during the Second World War, but when peace returned the decline in trade continued. From the 1920s there was little new building in the area and Butetown became run down. Most of the Bute Estate's housing of the 1850s was demolished in the early 1960s to make way for council housing, the Floor of the Coal Exchange closed in 1958, and coal exports from the port ceased in 1964, the year the Bute West Dock closed. This was followed, in 1970, by the closure of the Bute East Dock, which has been shortened and incorporated into the Atlantic Wharf development which includes the new County Hall. However, the future looks brighter for Butetown, for, after years of neglect, ambitious plans are being made to regenerate the area.

Future Plans for Butetown and the Docks

Butetown is changing rapidly to achieve an objective set by the Secretary of State: *'To reunite the city centre of Cardiff with its Waterfront'*. The main developments which will affect the area covered in this walk are:

The Barrage - this will run for three quarters of a mile, from just inside the Queen Alexandra Dock entrance across to Penarth Head. The Barrage will exclude the sea and its forty foot tides, and the tidal mudflats will be submerged under a 500 acre non-tidal freshwater lake, fed by the rivers Taff and Ely. Construction of the Barrage began in the summer of 1994 and is expected to take four and a half years.

The Peripheral Distributor Road (PDR) - is an eighteen and a half mile long dual-carriageway which will link Cardiff and the Bay directly to the M4. The 'Butetown Link' section of the PDR crosses the River Taff and passes underground for almost half a mile, before emerging near the Inner Harbour.

Mount Stuart Square - there are plans to develop a new Square, containing more offices and shops, as an extension to the north-west corner of Mount Stuart Square.

Roath Basin - plans here are for a development known as Capital Waterside, which will include offices, houses and apartments, a hotel, shops, restaurants, parks, and a 2,000-seat National Opera House.

Catch a train from Queen Street Station to Cardiff Bay Station (no service on Sundays) or bus number 7. If you catch the bus, get off at the top of West Bute Street and walk back to Cardiff Bay Station.

This three-storeyed building is the only survivor from a large group of buildings erected as the headquarters of the Taff Vale Railway Company in 1842. Bute Road Station, which was the terminus of their line from Merthyr Tydfil, is one of the earliest purpose-built railway buildings still standing. From 1862 the building housed a number of foreign consulates and later the offices of Cardiff's Port Manager. In 1981 the station became an unstaffed halt and was acquired by the Butetown Historic Railway Society. Until recently the ground floor housed the Welsh Industrial and Maritime Museum's Railway Gallery.

Cross Bute Street at the pedestrian crossing and turn left. A little further, on the corner, is the green building, 126 Bute Street (1).

This is part of a terrace built in the late 1840s by Hemingway and Pearson, the company who later constructed the Bute East Dock. The terrace was known as Britannia Buildings because Hemingway and Pearson also constructed the Britannia Bridge over the Menai Straits in North Wales at about the same time. For a time the building was occupied by the ship chandlers, Joseph Frazer and Company. It was purchased by the Welsh Industrial and Maritime Museum in 1982.

Take the right hand fork, with the Royal Bank of Scotland on your left, and walk along West Bute Street. On the right hand side, after the car park, is Cymric Buildings (2).

The site of Cymric Buildings was originally occupied by a terrace of cottages. These were acquired by the shipowners Griffin and Tatum in 1911 and demolished to build Cymric Buildings, designed by Henry Budgen. In 1939 the office block was bought by the Great Western Railway. There are some interesting stone carvings on a maritime theme decorating this building.

Opposite Cymric Buildings is the small, cream-coloured Bute Dock Hotel (3).

This is thought to be the oldest building in Butetown and is the only remaining example of cottage-style architecture in the area. It opened in 1839, at the same time as the first dock, after which it is named.

Next door to the Bute Dock Hotel is the National Westminster Bank (4).

This building, designed by F.C.R. Palmer and W.F.C. Holden, is one of the

National Westminster (Provincial) Bank 1929

largest and most imposing in the docks, and used to be known as the 'Shipowners' Memorial'. When it was built, in 1927, it was the largest bank outside London. Like most of the buildings in the Civic Centre it is built of Portland stone. The bronze figure over the doorway is a replica of the work of J.A. Stevenson, originally exhibited at the Royal Academy. It represents Equity. On one side of the scales is the Mercury head, a standard bank weight.

Turn right opposite the National Westminster Bank into Mount Stuart Square.

Mount Stuart Square was built on the site of a glassworks, situated next to the Glamorganshire Canal. The glassworks was operated by the Guest family who owned the Dowlais Iron Company at Merthyr Tydfil.

Mount Stuart Square was envisaged by the Second Marquis of Bute as a Square of elegant town houses, overlooking a central garden - a district for professional people. The Square was developed between 1855 and 1860 and three styles of houses were built. From the 1880s the character of Mount Stuart Square changed from residential to commercial as the Square became the centre of the coal trade, and residents moved out to quieter suburbs, such as Roath, Canton, and Splott. Vacated houses were converted into offices, and, in 1884-6, the transformation was completed when the Coal and Shipping Exchange was built on the gardens in the middle of the Square. From the late 1920s, with the collapse of the coal export trade after the First World War, there was little new building in Mount Stuart Square. The Square became run down and some houses, mainly on the west side, were demolished in the 1950s and 60s. In 1981 Mount Stuart Square was designated a Conservation Area by Cardiff City Council and steps have since been taken to improve its appearance.

On the corner is St. Stephen's Church (5).

This church, which contains a stained glass window from the London studio of William Morris, was designed by E.M. Bruce Vaughan and built in 1902. It replaced a temporary iron church, erected in 1878 as a chapel-of-ease to St. Mary's on Bute Street. In 1912 St. Stephen's was made a parish church. The building has now been adapted for use by a commercial organisation.

On the right hand side, opposite St. Stephen's Church, is Cambrian Buildings (6).

Cambrian Buildings has the same style of decoration as Cymric Buildings. Indeed, they look as though they are part of the same building, but they were developed separately. Cambrian Buildings stands on the former site of the Bute Town National School. When the school closed in 1907, the site was sold to a syndicate consisting of the shipowners, Henry Griffin and William Tatem, and the architect, Henry Budgen. In 1910 the present building was erected, designed by Budgen. It was named after the Cambrian Trust Ltd, a colliery concern, who bought it.

The next building on the right is Beynon House (7).

Originally named Baltic Buildings, Beynon House was built in 1900 and housed iron-ore importers and ship-brokers. The stone plaques on the front of the building depict the historical development of ships from the sailing-galley with oars to the earliest steam ships. By 1911 the building had been renamed Atlantic Buildings, and then, in 1939, the building was bought by the South American Saint Line Shipping Company and renamed Saint Line House. Beynon House is a recent name.

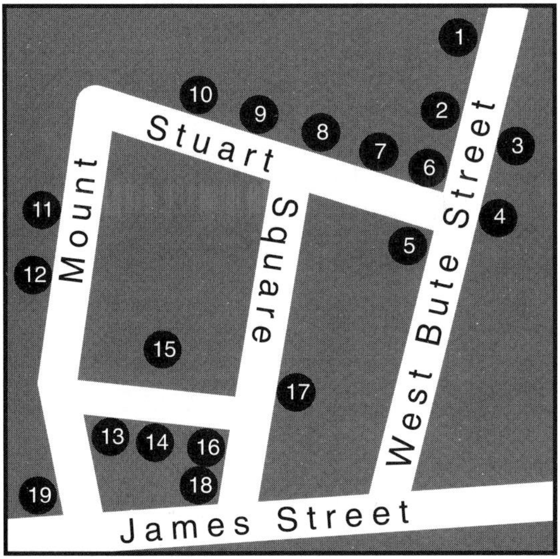

Next to Beynon House are two houses (numbers 58 and 59) (8).

These three-storey houses show the style of the second phase of house building in the Square - slightly wider than the first-phase buildings, with plain moulding around the doors and windows. The three-storey houses in the Square had a rear extension to the ground floor containing a closet and wash-house, and a cellar which housed the kitchen and scullery.

Empire House is the next building on the right (9).

Empire House was designed by Jones and Thomas and built in 1926 for the present owners and principal occupiers, the Evans and Reid Coal Company. Water was discovered during the excavations for the foundations of this building, which had to extend thirty-seven feet below pavement level. This was a common problem with many of the larger buildings built in the area.

The house on the end is number 53 (10).

The original development of Mount Stuart Square began on the north-western side of the Square, and number 53 is the only remaining example of the style of the first phase of house building. This plain, two-storey Georgian-style house was built in 1855. It has a width of eighteen and a half feet, compared with later houses in the Square, which were twenty feet wide. Originally this house had two rooms on each floor and a detached wash-house and privy. Additions to this building were approved in 1899.

Follow the road round to the left. The first building on the right hand side is number 34, Imperial House, and next door is number 33 (11).

These two houses are the sole survivors of a block of nineteen houses built along the northern and western sides of the Square. These three-storey houses, with the scallop design over the windows, are examples of the final design adopted for the town houses in the Square.

The next building on the right, after the car park is Aberdare House (12).

This is a very elegant house with curved windows and fine stone-carving. Rebuilt from two houses in 1920, it was designed by Henry Budgen for a firm of colliery owners, D.R. Llewellyn, Merret and Price Ltd.

Take the next turning on the left. On the right is number 23, Marine House, and next door is number 20 (13).

These recently renovated houses are more examples of the final design for the town houses in the Square, as the scallop design over the windows indicates.

Next door is Baltic House (14).

Designed by Henry Budgen, this building occupies the site of three original Mount Stuart Square houses and a Welsh Independent chapel. Plans were approved to build offices on this site in 1913, but because of the war they were not completed until 1920. Detailed engraving on the building portrays galleons and steam boats. It is now the headquarters of the Cardiff Bay Development Corporation.

On the left hand side is the Exchange (15).

The Coal and Shipping Exchange was built on the gardens in the middle of Mount Stuart Square, on the site of the former glassworks. The foundations of the building were very difficult to lay because there were pits still remaining from the glassworks and the subsoil was sticky clay to a depth of nine metres.

Designed by James, Seward, and Thomas, the Exchange was built between 1884-6. Before the Exchange opened, business was conducted in the open around the pierhead, or, if the weather was inclement, in the local pubs. In 1911-12 the Coal Exchange was extensively rebuilt and the Floor was reconstructed entirely in wood to reflect its commercial importance. The Coal Exchange Floor

The Exchange

was where South Wales steam coal prices were fixed between 11am and 1pm, and the buying, selling, and transporting of coal and other cargoes were negotiated. In its heyday the economy of the world was run from this Floor, and it was said that when standing on the Floor you could reach out in any direction and touch the shoulder of a millionaire.

Activity reached a peak in 1913, then the decrease in coal exports during the Depression led to a decline in business at the Coal Exchange, and the close of the dealing Floor in 1958. A period of neglect followed and the building fell into disrepair.

In 1971, the Exchange was bought by Control Securities who tried to rejuvenate it. It was during this period that the bombproof underground carpark was constructed which has ruined the front of the building. In 1977 it was suggested that the building should be used to house the Welsh Assembly, but this plan was abandoned. Now owned by the Cardiff Bay Development Corporation, this Grade II listed building is used for television and film productions, and as a venue for plays, concerts, and antique fairs. It is possible to go onto the Floor and look around. Go through the doors to the left of the main entrance and ask at the reception desk there.

Walk to the end of the road. On the right hand corner is Gloucester House (16).

In 1892 the Gloucester Bank built a new branch here and called the building Gloucester Chambers. From 1897 the building was used as offices, until heavy snow damaged the roof in 1982. The building deteriorated until it was demolished in 1987 to build Gloucester House, designed by Andrew Parker Associates. This was the first new building in the Square since Empire House was built in 1926.

Ahead are house numbers 6-9 (17).

These four houses, which were originally part of a terrace of six, have recently been restored. They are further examples of the final design for town houses in the Square. Number 6 housed both the German consulate and the Brazilian vice-consulate in the 1880s, an indication of the cosmopolitan nature of the Square at that time. In 1889, number 9 was given a new facade and named after Sir William Perch, a colliery owner who lived there.

Turn right and walk to the end of the road.

The entrance to a new estate opposite incorporates a re-erected stone, salvaged from an earlier building on the site. The design on the stone is a scallop with the inscription 'Nonpareil Market 1885'.

The Ship and Pilot is on your right (18).

This pub was originally two cottages which were licenced in 1861 as the Ship and Pilot Hotel. In 1881 the present building was erected, designed by the architect E.W.M. Corbett. Eight years later the pub was leased to William Hancock and Company Ltd, a Cardiff brewery who bought it in 1926.

Turn right and walk along James Street. On the corner of Mount Stuart Square is Mount Stuart House (19).

This site originally contained two cottages fronting James Street. The present building, designed by H.T. Thornley, was built in 1898 and became the offices of John Cory and Sons Ltd. Cory was a shipowner who moved to Cardiff from Devon in 1872. The company owned ships until 1966, but is now a travel agency and freight forwarder.

On the left is Imperial House (20).

This building, which used to be called Merthyr House, was built between 1911 and 1916 by the Bute Docks Building and Office Company. It was an important building at one time, occupied by various shipping companies. In 1946 a fire destroyed the front part of the building together with records of most of the old shipping companies in the docks. A new facade was built in the 1960s, in typical sixties style and totally out of character with the elegant style of the original building, which can still be seen from behind the building. Now the building is derelict and deteriorating.

Merthyr House c.1929

Turn left before Imperial House and walk along Adelaide Street. Turn left at the T-junction and walk to the large cream building, The Big Windsor (21).

The Big Windsor was originally a nickname for the Windsor Hotel, used to distinguish it from the smaller Windsor Arms across the road. The building, which was first licenced in 1855, was largely rebuilt in 1882. The Big Windsor was renowned in the post-war era for serving the best food in Cardiff - a feat commemorated by a plaque beside the door to Abel Magneron, the chef. Today the building is a Grade II listed building.

On the other corner of the road is the Pilotage building (22).

There is some contention about the history of this building which was built in the early 1860s. Bricked up archways at the rear gave rise to the theory that the building had been built as stables for the Marquis of Bute's horses when the early docks were being built. Others believe that the building was constructed as offices for the Pilotage Authority who occupied it from the 1870s. Pilotage was very important in the Bristol Channel because of the massive forty foot tidal range. The Pilotage Board, which licenced and trained pilots, was formally set up at Bristol in 1807, and established in Cardiff in 1861. Cardiff then became the premier port of the channel, and by 1883 there were 110 pilots operating from this office. It was only in 1988 that the South Wales Pilotage Authority vacated the Pilotage building. Now the building is the headquarters of the Cardiff Bay Art Trust and houses occasional exhibitions.

Turn right between the Big Windsor and the Pilotage building and walk towards Landsea House ahead, which used to be part of the dry docks complex. Turn right and go through the blue gates to the dry docks.

The dry, or graving, docks developed from the Mount Stuart Graving Dock, which was established by John Batchelor in 1853. It was ideally situated and expanded rapidly, so that by the turn of the century there were two further dry docks in operation, capable of handling much larger vessels. In 1872, the concern was taken over by Charles Hill and Sons. Ship building was never a major industry at Cardiff for several reasons: lack of space; high yard rents; competition from established yards in England; and indifferent marine engineering facilities. However, in the nineteenth century Cardiff was one of the primary ship-repair ports in the world.

Turn left and follow the path beside the black railings to the wooden benches at the end.

Here there are good views across the Bristol Channel and to Penarth Head. The proposed Barrage will extend between the two headlands. The islands, Flatholme and Steepholme, which are geologically a continuation of the Mendips, can also be seen on a clear day.

Follow the path right round to the grey building on your left. This is Q-shed (23).

Q-shed was built in 1871 as a booking office for the Cardiff and Bristol Channel steamships. The last regular commercial service from this point was in 1916 and the pleasure trips which used to leave from Q-shed were discontinued in the late 1970s. In 1987 Q-shed was converted into the museum's Maritime Gallery. Now it is used for museum events and activities.

The wooden structures just off-shore near Q-shed are called dolphins. At one time the P. & A. Campbell paddle steamers, known as the 'White Funnel Fleet', sailed regularly from these dolphins. This famous fleet began in 1887, when the brothers Peter and Alec Campbell brought their steamer 'Waverley' from the Clyde to Bristol. It was in Bristol that the pair developed their own repair yard and administrative centre, building their fleet up to thirteen vessels which sailed to all parts of the Bristol Channel. The signals were erected to indicate which berth vessels were to moor at. The Campbells ceased trading in the 1950s, but it is still possible to take a pleasure trip on one of the two steamers, 'Balmoral' and 'Waverley', that cruise the channel in the summer months.

Go through the black wrought iron gate and turn right. Walk behind the Welsh Industrial and Maritime Museum (24).

The site of the main museum building was originally six houses which were demolished in 1885 to build a Merchants' Exchange. In 1892 a major fire nearly destroyed the Merchants' Exchange, but it was rebuilt in 1895 and bought by Powell Dyffryn, the largest colliery company in South Wales, as their headquarters. The building, a three-storey, red brick building with high curving gables, was renamed Powell Dyffryn House. In the early 1970s the building was acquired by the museum who demolished it to build this modern purpose-built gallery, designed by H.M.R. Burgess and partners. The building opened in 1977.

Continue, over the wooden walkway.

This walkway crosses the entrance to the filled-in Bute West Dock, the first dock to be built, in 1839. In the area to your left, which houses the outdoor museum exhibits, the kerb-stones at the edge of the entrance basin to the West Dock can be clearly seen. The dock closed in 1964 and was landfilled in 1970.

The next building, the Pierhead Building (25), may look like a sand sculpture but it has survived the elements for nearly a hundred years.

This imposing French Gothic terracotta building, situated to impress the shipping traffic, was built in 1896 as offices for the Bute Dock Company. A year later, after receiving permission to construct its own railways to link the docks with the mining valleys, the company changed its name to the Cardiff Railway Company. This association is signified in the panel on the west side of the building, showing a ship, a train, and the coats of arms of the old borough and the Bute family. The motto beneath: 'Wrth Ddwr a Than' means 'With water and fire'. A similar motto is incorporated into the mosaic floor in the reception foyer inside the building. From 1923 to 1947 the building was the headquarters of the Great Western Railway, the largest independent dock owner at that time. The lavish skyline is reminiscent of the architectural style of William Burges. In fact the architect was William Frame, Burges's apprentice who completed work at Cardiff Castle and Castell Coch after Burges's death. The Pierhead Building, a Grade I listed building, is now the administrative office for the Port of Cardiff which is run by Associated British Ports.

The entrance to Bute West Dock with the Pierhead Building in the background

Continue past the Pierhead Building on the promenade alongside the inner harbour until you reach the castellated building on your left (26).

This building, until recently the headquarters of the customs' services, was sighted fifty metres to the north of its present position. Moved in its entirety to allow the construction of the new NCM Credit building, it will now be preserved.

Continue along the promenade until you reach the Norwegian Church (27).

The original Norwegian church was the first to be established outside Norway by the Norwegian Maritime Mission. It was built in 1868 of corrugated iron, and remained the place of worship for Cardiff's immigrant Scandinavian community until the 1950s. Roald Dahl, the famous author of children's stories, was baptised in the church. In 1971 the church was deconsecrated and fell into disrepair. The new church is a replica of the original.

Turn left as you leave the Norwegian Church and follow the walkway to the Roath Basin and the moored Goleulong 2000 Lightship (28).

In 1856 a tidal harbour south of the Bute Docks was opened. An increase in coal production after the exploitation of the Rhondda Valley in the 1860s meant that the two Bute Docks were inadequate, and in 1874 the tidal harbour was converted into the Roath Basin. The Roath Dock, which opened in 1887, is connected to the Roath Basin by a lock. These docks, and the larger Queen Alexandra Dock to the south, are still in use. Moored in the entrance to the Roath Basin is the former Trinity House Lightship, The Helwick, which until the late eighties was stationed off Rhossili Point on the Gower Coast. The Helwick has now been transformed into a floating Christian Centre and renamed Goleulong 2000

Next to the Lightship is the Cardiff Bay Visitor Centre (29).

This tube-shaped building houses a free exhibition outlining the plans for the regeneration of Cardiff's docklands. When it opened in 1991, this building won a commendation in the Sunday Times Royal Fine Art Commission's Building of the Year competition. The architects were Alsop, Lyall, and Stormer.

When you leave the Visitor Centre, follow the esplanade back to the Pierhead Building. The ironstone ledge on your right has carvings, inlaid rocks, and paintings on a sea theme. Continue to the Maritime Museum and then turn right along Bute Street until you reach Cardiff Bay Station where you began your walk.

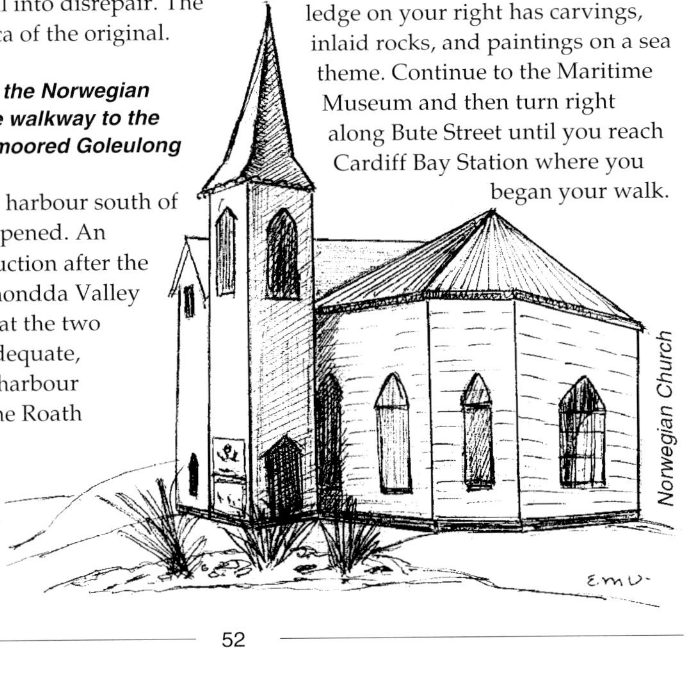

Norwegian Church

Pierhead Building

BIBLIOGRAPHY

The following books and leaflets were used in the compilation of this book:

Books:

Morgan, D. (1991). *The Cardiff Story.* D. Brown & Sons Limited.

Hilling, J.B. (1991). *Shire County Guide - Glamorgan*. Shire Publications Limited.

Hilling, J.B. (1969). *"The buildings of Cardiff: an historical survey"* . In Stewart Williams' Glamorgan Historian, Volume 6. D. Brown & Sons Limited.

Hilling, J.B. (1978). *Llandaf Past and Present*. Stewart Williams, Barry.

Parker, M. & Carter, N. (1989). *Butetown: A visitors guide*. Survey of Cardiff Occasional Paper No.2.

The Survey of Cardiff. (1989). The inner harbour: an historical appraisal. A report prepared for the Cardiff Bay Development Corporation.

Aberdare Hall - One of the buildings to be found during Walk 2, The Civic Centre

Leaflets:

"Llandaff circular walk". Merthyr and Cynon Groundwork Trust.

"Llandaff: a brief history". Llandaff Society.

"Cardiff: the old town wall". Cardiff City Council.

"Cardiff: a history of the Civic Centre". Cardiff City Council.

"Cardiff: the Central Market". Cardiff City Council.

"Cardiff Castle". (From the castle shop)

"The old library: exhibitions, art and craft at the centre of the city". City of Cardiff.

"City Hall". City of Cardiff.

"Three castles cycle route: Cardiff Castle to Castell Coch". County of South Glamorgan.

"Butetown walkabout". Welsh Industrial and Maritime Museum.

"The Parish church of Cardiff: St. John the Baptist". (From the church)

"Europe's most exciting waterfront development". Cardiff Bay Development Corporation.

"The history and development of the port of Cardiff". (From the Pierhead Building).

"Cardiff Bay: building a quality environment". Cardiff Bay Development Corporation.

In addition - newspaper and magazine articles, unpublished material from the City of Cardiff's Leisure and Amenities Department.